ANI

ESSAYS

WRITERS SERIES 27

SERIES EDITORS:

ANTONIO D'ALFONSO AND JOSEPH PIVATO

Canada Council
for the Arts

Conseil des Arts
du Canada

Guernica Editions Inc. acknowledges the support
of the Canada Council for the Arts.

ANNE HÉBERT

ESSAYS ON HER WORKS

EDITED BY LEE SKALLERUP

GUERNICA
TORONTO – BUFFALO – LANCASTER (U.K.)
2010

Lee Skallerup, Guest editor
Guernica Editions Inc.
P.O. Box 117, Station P, Toronto (ON), Canada M5S 2S6
2250 Military Road, Tonawanda, N.Y. 14150-6000 U.S.A.

Distributors:
University of Toronto Press Distribution,
5201 Dufferin Street, Toronto (ON), Canada M3H 5T8
Gazelle Book Services, White Cross Mills, High Town,
Lancaster LA1 4XS U.K.

First edition.
Printed in Canada.

Legal Deposit – Third Quarter
Library of Congress Catalog Card Number: 2009926623
Library and Archives Canada Cataloguing in Publication
Anne Hébert : essays on her works / edited by Lee Skallerup.
(Writers series ; 27)
Includes bibliographical references.
ISBN 978-1-55071-278-0
1. Hébert, Anne, 1916-2000 — Criticism and interpretation.
I. Skallerup, Lee, 1977- II. Series: Writers series (Toronto, Ont.) ; 27
PS8515.E16Z5493 2009   C843'.54   C2009-902310-5

Contents

Acknowledgements 6

Introduction: Anne Hébert in Darkness and in Light
    by Lee Skallerup 7

Hébert's Uncanny: Death and "Radical Speech"
    in *Le Tombeau des rois* by Robert David Stacey 19

Re-Writing Women's Destinies in Anne Hébert's *La
    Cage* and *L'Île de la Demoiselle*
    by Elodie Rousselot 39

The Red Dress in Hébert's Late Novels
    by Deborah Hamilton 70

Chacun son diable: Anne Hébert's Lucifer
    by Annabelle M. Rea 95

Transgendered Identities in Anne Hébert's *Un habit
    de lumière* and Almódovar's *All About My Mother*
    by Bénédicte Mauguière 116

"J'habite la fièvre et la démence, comme mon pays
    natal": Love-Triangle as Political Allegory in
    Kamouraska by Lee Skallerup 138

Anne Hébert Interview by Michel Gosselin 161

Biography of Anne Hébert 171

Bibliography for Anne Hébert 175

Contributors 182

Acknowledgements

I would like to thank Joseph Pivato of Guernica Editions for suggesting that I do this book in the first place. His patience and support have been invaluable. I would also like to thank my supervisor, Lynn Penrod, for allowing me to work on this project simultaneously to working on my dissertation. Christiane Bisson and Nathalie Watteyne from the Centre Anne-Hébert were invaluable to my research efforts. Also, I am indebted to Richard Giguère, who introduced me to Hébert's poems many years ago while I was an undergraduate at the Universté de Sherbrooke. Finally this book never would have been completed if not for the love and support of my husband Murray Bessette.

I would like to dedicate this book to my late grandmother, Mildred Blair. Sorry I couldn't get it done faster, Nanny.

Introduction: Anne Hébert

In Darkness and in Light

Lee Skallerup

Upon Anne Hébert's death in January 2000, there was an outpouring of tributes across Canada and around the world. *The New York Times* obituary credited Hébert with "[breathing] new life into fading language" in Quebec and beyond, as well as "[bringing] the violent passions of her native rural Quebec to wider audiences in France and the United States" (Brooke C26). Newspapers and news magazines around Europe mourned the passing of one of the most important figures of Quebec literature. Authors in both English and French in Canada described with great affection the influence the author had on their writings. Perhaps the most eloquent description of Hébert and her work came from her translator, Sheila Fischman, and appeared in *Maclean's* magazine soon after her death:

> She ventured into the darkest, most violent areas of the human soul, yet she makes us acknowledge that the darkness, even the violence, are part of our condition and that we must accept them if we hope to know ourselves . . .
>
> In everything she wrote, Hebert used the French lan-

guage like something fine and rare; her style is never precious or pretentious, but luminous and pure. Every word she used was necessary and right. And her prose as well as her poetry is lyrical and harmonious . . . (Fischman 57).

Anne Hébert's literary career spanned over half a century and includes poetry, novels, short stories, plays and even a light opera for children. She has won almost every major literary award from Canada and France, including three Governor General's Awards, the Prix Fémina and the Molson Prize. Many felt she should have won a Nobel Prize for the body of her work.

Hébert's first collection of poems, *Les Songes en équilibre*, appeared in 1942. Over the next ten years, her poetic vision would refine itself under the shadow of "La Grande Noirceur," a period of intense repression and censorship in Quebec. As a child, Hébert was free to explore a variety of literary influences; as a young adult, she discovered that this freedom was not universal. *Le Torrent*, a collection of five short stories, featured a dark and disturbing vision of the family, religion and rural Quebec. Despite strong reviews, Hébert had difficulty finding a publisher for her second collection of poems *Le Tombeau des rois*. In 1953, the collection was published privately at a great cost to the author and as a result in 1954, Hébert moved to Paris to finish her first novel, settling there permanently in 1965 upon the death of her mother.

Le Torrent and *Le Tombeau des rois* introduce the reader to the themes and images that will populate Hébert's literary landscape throughout her oeuvre.

The title story of *Le Torrent* is the tale of a troubled relationship between mother and son, and their lasting effects. The simple opening lines of the novel not only introduce the reader to the main character, but also to the sparse poetic style and haunting images that populate Hébert's literary world: "J'étais un enfant dépossédé monde. Par le décret d'une volonté antérieure à la mienne, je devais renoncer à toute possession en cette vie. Je touchais au monde par fragments..." (*Le Torrent* 19). It is the limited perspective of the child taken to the extreme and in this case, limited as a result of his mother's actions. The child would figure prominently in many of Hébert's works: the young girl who makes the journey down to *Le Tombeau des rois*, Catherine, Michel and Lia's traumatic childhoods in *Les chambres de bois*, the murdered girls who wander the shores in *Les Fous de Bassan*, the haunted children of *Les Enfants du sabbat*, the sheltered childhoods of Julien and Hélène that appear in *L'enfant chargé des songes*, the isolation and awakening of Aurélien in *Aurélien, Clara, Mademoiselle et le Lieutenant anglais* and finally the sexual questioning of young Miguel in *Un habit de lumière*. Each one of these children that Hébert has created could have uttered the line: "J'étais un enfant dépossédé du monde."

Hébert has also probed the question of religion in her works, more specifically how religion can be used to oppress rather than to liberate. François, the young boy in *Le Torrent*, is at the mercy of his mother and is made to pay for her sins, namely having a child outside of wedlock: "Il faut se dompter jusqu'aux os. On

9

n'a pas idée de la force mauvaise qui est en nous! Tu m'entends, François? Je te dompterai bien, moi . . ." (*Le Torrent* 20). In the title poem of *Le Tombeau des rois*, the young girl is prepared to be sacrificed before the seven dead kings: "Avides de la source fraternelle de mal en moi/Ils me couchent et me boivent;/Sept fois, je connais l'étau des os/Et la main sèche qui cherche le coeur pour le rompre" (*Oeuvre poétique* 54). Religion is a tool of fear, rather than salvation in Hébert's universe. Although seemingly a direct reference to the dominant Catholic Church in Quebec, Hébert encouraged readers to look beyond the borders of her home province: "Je m'étonne quand la critique décrit *Le Torrent* comme le symbole du Québec enchaîné. C'est une abstraction. Il faudrait plutôt s'interroger sur la fonction de la mère, de la religion, ce sont des problèmes essentiels du moins en ce qui me concerne" (Vanasse 446).

This "essentiel" trait that Hébert encourages the reader to look for in her works often troubled critics. In the 1950's, Quebec was beginning to emerge from what was known as "La grande noirceur" and moving into "the Quiet Revolution." People were looking for voices to represent this transition, and Hébert's collection *Le Tombeau des rois* provided a poetic vision that for many articulated the transition that Quebec was experiencing. *Le dictionnaire des oeuvres littéraires du Québec* offers this type of nationalistic interpretation of *Le Tombeau des rois*:

Mais la grande poésie se montre capable non seulement de recueillir mais aussi de faire crouler l'expérience *com-*

mune enfouie en la mémoire…Un tel renversement, celui qu'opère *le Tombeau des rois*, est proprement *historique* même s'il a pu passer presque inaperçu malgré les critiques louangeuses qui revelaient en fait la fusion réussie d'une écriture toute personnelle et *d'une préoccupation collective*. Il est enfin significatif que cet exploit, comme le signale Pierre Emmanuel, le préfacier, s'opère *"à Quebec,"* en cette capitale, défavorisée par tant de séquelles *coloniales ou cléricales* et qui regagne ainsi – comme avec Saint-Denys Garneau, Alain Grandbois et Roger Lemelin – quelque chose du leadership littéraire ancien qu'elle avait perdu (Lemieux 1001, emphasis added).

Hébert's insistence on a more universal interpretation would run contrary to many Quebec critics, and as Eva-Marie Kröller observes, many nationalist critics "were sharply critical of Hébert's introspective work which they…[characterized] as insufferably morbid and therefore unsupportive of the separatist cause" (Kröller 6). *Kamouraska* would provide nationalist critics in Quebec much to work with, as Elisabeth abandons her French husband for an English doctor. When her husband is murdered and Elisabeth is accused of plotting the crime with her English lover, the accusation comes from an English judge, who is ruling on behalf of the Queen of England. Simultaneously, there are references to the Rébellion des Patriots, as well as the changing landscape of North America. Some have criticized the novel for being too much of a tragic love story and not enough of a political statement concerning the oppression the French faced at the hands of the English. The novel is based in part on a true story, and was a part of Hébert's family mythology, having grown up listening to her mother telling the story of her ill-fated ancestor Achille Taché. The story fascinated Hébert, and she once again creates a character whose childhood was sheltered and oppressive, and looks to an ideal love as an escape, leading only to tragedy. Regardless of the novel's political meaning, Hébert creates a complex world full of passion and sadness, and as put by Kröller: "The book remains an elegant, passionate and unsparing account of human frailty, and it is as vivid an evocation of the place and period it describes as is likely to come our way" (8).

Kröller also points to another critical challenge that Hébert's emphasis on the "essentiel" posed: as the nationalist critics in the 1950s, 1960s and 1970s looked to Hébert to provide a voice for Quebec, the 1980s saw feminists look to Hébert as a voice for women. Patricia Smart was one of the first critics to offer a new feminine/feminist reading of the collection of poems in an article entitled "La poésie d'Anne Hébert: une perspective féministe." Studying the first three collections of Anne Hébert's poetry, Smart states:

> . . . livre une nouvelle cohérence et une portée autrement lorsque [l'oeuvre poétique d'Anne Hébert] est regardée selon une perspective féminine. Les traits spécifiques de la féminité tels que définis par Clément, Cixous et d'autres – monde renversé porteur d'un nouvel ordre, subversion instaurée par le regard d'une enfant sauvage, affirmation de la puissance d'Éros contre le pouvoir répressif du Logos – sont en effet les clefs de voûte de l'univers hébertien" (Smart 178).

Specifically, in dealing with *Le Tombeau des rois*, Smart points out how Hébert uses the image of the house as not just a "symbole abstrait de l'isolement et de l'enfermement" but instead as "l'habitation d'une femme onirique, sorte de Rapunzel liée à son sort par un décret de fidélité antérieur de sa volonté" (181). Hébert questions and problematizes traditionally "female" jobs such as setting the table ("La chambre fermée"), sewing ("Le chambre de bois") and even cleaning ("La fille maigre," "Une petite morte") by pairing them off with bizarre and morbid imagery:

> Qui donc a pris la juste mesure
> De la croix tremblante de mes bras étendus?
> . . .
> Mon coeur sur la table posé,
> Qui donc a mis le couvert avec soin
> Affilé le petit couteau . . . (*Oeuvre poétique* 35)

Smart also speaks of Hébert's critique of the matriarchy, that "perpétu[e] le règne de la mort en prêchant la douceur et la perte de soi" (178), illustrated in the final verses of the poem "Les pêcheurs d'eau":

> Tout l'arbre droit,
> Et l'oiseau,
> Cette espèce de roi
> Miniscule et naïf.
> Et puis, aussi,
> Cette femme qui coud
> Au pied de l'arbre
> Sous le coup de midi

Cette femme assise
Refait, point à point,
L'humilité du monde,
Rien qu'avec la douce patience
De ses deux mains brûlées. (*Oeuvre poétique* 16)

Here, we see not only the subversion of traditionally "female" acts, but we also note that the woman, despite being visibly harmed, remains a passive, tiny king (a female trying to be male) and maintains the status quo. Victim of this preached passivity, the narrator is led to the final poem where:

. . . la passivité féminine est amenée à son ultime et plus terrible conséquence: le consentement au viol. La rencontre de la mort est vécue comme une noce étrange, exorcisme peut-être des derniers relents de masochisme dans la psyché féminine. Il est significatif que la victime soit préparée au sacrifice par « l'ombre de l'amour ? », et que sa libération coïncide avec l'introduction d'une figure fémine *active* – la chasseresse (182).

We can see through this re-reading how Hébert's collection of poems can quite readily lend itself to this more feminist interpretation.

Just as often as Hébert tried to divorce herself from the nationalist movement in Quebec, she also refuted any statement that she was a feminist (see Poulin, "Afterword," 154). Her heroines were as often complex and difficult to sympathize with as any antagonist, male or female. Elisabeth, in *Kamouraska*, held other women in contempt and displays a self-absorption bordering on farcical, while the women in her family are simplistic and unwilling or unable to create a family environment where Elisabeth can thrive. In fact, many of the antagonists in Hébert's novels are women, usually the mothers, who fail their children and help create the circumstances that lead to the protagonists' downfall. François' mother in *Le Torrent* may be a victim of the harsh religious oppression of her time, but it is difficult to sympathize with a character who writes in her daily list of things to do: "Battre François" (*Le Torrent* 21). Rose-Alba, the beautiful and shallow mother of Miguel in *Un habit de lumière*, may suffer in poverty and a loveless marriage, but her selfishness and vanity directly lead to her son's suicide. Hébert uses the trinity of female caricatures in her novels (the temptress, the virgin, the crone/mother) while simultaneously subverting and blurring the line between what these characterizations have traditionally represented. Hébert never shied away from exploring the darkness of the human condition, male or female.

In order to explore a character's inner self, Hébert would often use fantasy, the fantastic and the idea of "le songe." Translated as "dream" in all of her works, the English word does not carry the same weight as the French term, as expressed by Hébert herself to Frank Scott in a correspondence regarding his translations of the poem "Le Tombeau des rois": "*Dream*. Le français a deux mots, l'un de la vie courante: *rêve*, et l'autre, plus rare et littérare: *songe*. L'anglais n'a pas cette nuance" (*Dialogue* 58). It is unfortunate that no word in English exists as an equivalent to "songe," as the term appears in virtually all her works. There is also a sense of passivity to those who are experiencing the dreams, as in "Le Tombeau des rois": "(En quel songe/Cette enfant fut-elle liée par la cheville/Pareille à une esclave facinée?)" (*Oeuvre poétique* 52). These dreams are often nightmares, exposing the dark side of human nature: the demonic figures in *Les Enfants du sabbat*, the vampire in *Héloïse*, the dead husband who visits Elisabeth in her dreams or the dead girls who haunt Pastor Nicolas Jones in *Les Fous de Bassan*. As many of the characters that Hébert creates submit to what they believe to be an escape from their lives into a realm of fantasy and dreams, they quickly realize that it is nothing but an illusion hiding a nightmare. Perhaps this image is most clearly articulated in *Un habit de lumière*, where both mother and son find refuge in the fantastic world of the nightclub *Paradis perdu*, a world of artifice and pageantry, seduced by a performer, Jean-Ephrem de la Tour, a world that is ultimately revealed to be false and an illusion: "Le loft de Jean-Ephrem de la Tour ne brille plus, vaste et profond à perte de vue. Il est plein de noirceur dans tous les coins. Vide surtout à décourager de vivre" (*Un habit* 129). The darkness where Miguel had found refuge reveals itself to be ultimately vacuous and empty, causing him to seek out a suit of light.

Un habit de lumière would mark the end of Hébert's long and illustrious literary career. But as she observed in an interview: "Depuis *Le Torrent* mon langage n'a pas dévié" (Morrissette 54). It serves as an interesting comparison, looking at the title story from *Le Torrent* alongside her final novel. *Un habit de lumière* does represent a new direction in Hébert's writing. The Almevida family is her first family not of

French origin, and Miguel's transgender identity is also new ground for Hébert. However, both share a similar structure to the story: part one deals with the young boy and how the relationship with his mother has shaped him, part two with the impact the mother-son relationship has on a romantic one. Both stories take place in relative poverty and under the shadow of Catholicism. Echoes can also be found in Hébert's final novel of *Le Tombeau des rois*. In *Un habit de lumière*, Miguel asks the following: "Qui donc m'a conduit jusqu'ici? Me tirant par la main, me poussant aux épaules, m'emmenant là où je m'étais juré de ne plus jamais revenir?" (125). In *Le Tombeau des rois*, one of the poems observes:

> Il y a certainement quelqu'un
> Qui m'a tuée
> Puis s'en est allé
> Sur la pointe des pieds
> Sans romper sa danse parfaite (*Oeuvre poétique* 44)

And in the title poem:

> Quel fil d'Ariane me mène
> Au long des dédales sourds?
> L'écho des pas s'y mange à mesure.
> ...
> L'auteur du songe
> Presse le fil,
> Et viennent les pas nus
> Un à un
> Comme les premières gouttes de pluie
> Au fond du puits. (*Oeuvre poétique* 52)

Much like the classic tragedy, the two boys, François and Miguel, are suffering for the sins of those who came before them, powerless, despite their best efforts, to overcome their fates. Someone has certainly led the characters to their ends. In a like manner, Hébert has both led the reader through a labyrinth of language throughout her oeuvre, and woven a suit of light for us to enjoy.

WORKS CITED

Brooke, James. "Anne Hébert, 83, Poet and Novelist of Quebec," *New York Times* Feb 3 2000: C26.

Fischman, Sheila. "A Literary Gem Cutter," *Maclean's* 113.6 (1999): 67.

Kröller, Eva-Marie. "Anne Hébert: 1916-2000," *Canadian Literature* 165 (2000): 5-8.

Lemieux, Pierre-Hervé. "Le Tombeau des rois." *Dictionnaire des oeuvres littéraires du Québec.* Tome III. Montreal: Fides, 1978.

Smart, Patricia. "La poèsie d'Anne Hébert: une perspective féministe." *L'autre lecture: La critique au féminin et les textes québécois."* Tome 1. Ed. Lori Saint-Martin. Montreal: XYZ éditeur, 1992.

Poulin, Alfred Jr. "Afterword," *Anne Hébert: Selected Poems.* Trans. Alfred Poulin, Jr. Brockport: BOA Editions, 1987.

Morissette, Brigitte. "Lointaine et proche Anne Hébert," *Châtelaine* Dec 1986: 34.

Vanasse, André. "L'écriture et l'ambivalence," *Voix et Images* 7.3 (1982): 446.

For the complete Anne Hébert bibliography, please refer to the Bibliography at the end of the collection.

Hébert's Uncanny Death and "Radical Speech" in *Le Tombeau des rois*

ROBERT DAVID STACEY

> *What are these songs*
> *straining at sense –*
> *you the consequence?*
> Louis Zukofsky

Most critics of Anne Hébert's *Le Tombeau des rois* have, quite legitimately, read the collection in terms of its engagement with the idea of death. Beyond that, however, there appears to be little agreement as to either the motivations for or ramifications of that confrontation. A cloud of indecision seems to hover over the text's critical history. Delbert Russell, for instance, claims that the collection "completely transcends the personal level" making sense not on a realist plane, but at "a universal and mythic level" (32). Pierre-Hervé Lemieux, on the other hand, insists on positioning the poems precisely in the "real" world, no matter how tenuous their commitment to a shared or sharable reality: "Le receuil du *Tombeau des rois* privilégie donc l'attention réaliste portée à son plus haut point" (1978, 138). This distinction is a critical one as it dictates the lines along which disagreements concerning the poetic speaker's ultimate relationship with death are divided. Interestingly enough, the text's political dimension is likewise determined along these lines, as feminist and/or nationalist readers tend to approach the content as allegorical of an emancipatory political process, ascribing to the volume both an historio-cultural specificity as well as liberating conclusion whereby the speaker triumphs over death.[1]

In such readings, "death" symbolizes a cluster of negative factors which impinge on the well-being of the female speaker. The reduction of "death" to a symbolic antagonist is, I believe, unwarranted and accounts for a number of misreadings. Most importantly, this hermeneutic strategy elides the existential dimension and psychological potency of the poems, and in actuality undermines the political efficacy entailed therein. Though few critics have read the collection in relation to its psychological dynamics, such an approach would seem to be demanded by the poems themselves through their invocation of the "uncanny" which is exploited and transformed in order to articulate a radical notion of female subjectivity. Death, as the sign under which the uncanny is said to operate, is therefore not a symbol, but a metonym – not the speaker's adversary in a struggle from which she may emerge either victorious or vanquished, but the unavoidable *product* (both fortuitous and devastating) of a peculiar psychological quest.

The idea of the uncanny (Freud's *das unheimlich*) not only underpins the affective power *Le Tombeau des Rois*, but constitutes its basic *method* as well: in these poems, the uncanny is deployed as a means of addressing the dissolution of specific structures that are simultaneously restrictive and performative, inhibiting the speaker's expression and self-consciousness *as a woman,* but making possible her subjectivity in the first place. Needless to say, then, *Le Tombeau des rois* is resolutely ambiguous, the poems pervaded by an ambivalence that is itself the principal theme of the book. As will become clear, the uncanny is particularly suited to the expression of this ambivalence and, from the reader's point of view, to its theorization.

In his essay "Das Unheimlich" (1919) Freud speaks of the uncanny feeling as a "class of the terrifying," a "morbid anxiety" that "recalls that sense of helplessness sometimes experienced in dreams." It is produced in the subject when he suddenly confronts something he had previously known, but to which he had become "estranged through the process of repression" (148). Understood as the "return of the repressed," the uncanny frames those moments in which the subject's objective knowledge (and hence his status as unified subject) is put into question. Consequently, Freud cites as instances of the uncanny those elements which convey a loss of control, an undermining of the subject's authority, or the frustration of his believed-in autonomy. Epilepsy and madness therefore elicit the feeling of the uncanny because "the ordinary person sees in them the workings of forces hitherto unsuspected in his fellow man but which at the same time he is dimly aware of in a remote corner of his own being" (151). Likewise, "dismembered limbs, a severed head, a hand cut off at the wrist, feet which dance by themselves – all these have something peculiarly uncanny about them" (151), precisely because as severed parts of the body (which, as in the case of the dancing feet, are nevertheless animated) they represent aspects of the subject's mental life which have been similarly "cut off" but continue to perform (in some "remote corner of his being") without his knowledge or permission.

Since the mechanism of the uncanny is the "return of the repressed," it constitutes at its most basic level an inversion whereby the subject's normal intercourse with the world is disrupted: the basic "rules" which govern his life are overturned and he is thrown into an unreliable and unpredictable universe. The comfortable binaries (consciousness/unconsciousness, interior/exterior, self/other) break down; life becomes interstitial.

An uncanny effect is often easily produced by effacing the distinction between imagination and reality, such as when something we had hitherto regarded as imaginary appears before us in reality, or when a symbol takes over the full functions and significance of the thing it symbolizes, and so on. (152)

Accordingly, the "living dead," ghosts, monsters, and mutants are uncanny because they challenge our ability to make basic "distinctions" between categories of being.

It is the notion of the "double," however, that provides Freud with the most salient example of the uncanny in that it connects the ideas of repression and "category confusion" in a very tangible manner. The fear of the double "harkens back to particular phases in the evolution of the self-regarding feeling, a regression to a time when the ego was not yet sharply differentiated from the external world and from other persons" (143). During this stage "of primary narcissism" the notion of the double, if it exists as such, is innocuous, benign. The subject, since he has not yet distinguished himself from the rest of the world, sees himself everywhere in it. Once this stage has been passed, however, and the subject necessarily represses or simply forgets the multiplicity of his being, "the double takes on a different aspect . . . [H]e becomes the ghastly harbinger of death" (141). The double delivers a blow to the subject's faith in the unity of his being.[2]

One is forcibly struck by the number of these elements which appear among the twenty-seven poems of *Le Tombeau des rois*. Madness ("La Chambre fermée"), interstitiality ("Les pêcheurs d'eau"), dismemberment ("Nos mains au jardin"), living-death ("Il y a certainement quelqu'un"), and blindness ("Le Tombeau des rois") all appear in one form or another throughout the text. So too does the "double" manifest itself with regularity; it is one of the text's principal motifs and is responsible for much of Hébert's eeriest imagery. In "Vie de château," the speaker places herself in an abandoned "château d'ancêstres." The manor house is an empty shell; it no longer possesses the qualities which once made it a home. There is no "table ni feu / Ni poussière ni tapis" (64). The absence of those objects one might associate with an active, living place (the warmth of the fire, the food on the table) anticipates ghostly presences. True to the long tradition of the *unheimlich*, or haunted, house, they appear in the "polished mirrors" that alone give the place its "enchantement pervers":

Vois, ces glaces sont profondes
Comme des armoires
Toujours quelque mort y habite sous le tain
Et couvre aussitôt ton reflet
Se colle à toi comme une algue.

The mirror which should merely confirm the presence of the speaker to herself is "deep," containing a corpse behind the silvering which first covers her reflection and then moves beyond the mirror to "stick" to the speaker herself like an "algae."

"Vie de château" presents the double as an active force which, in the words of Freud, elicits fear when "the foreign self is substituted for [the subject's] own" (141). The double is paradoxically the subject and not the subject, her "plus dure image" but also something dead, "sans ombre ni couleur." Hence the "perversity" of the final two lines, in which the speaker's mirror image "S'ajuste a toi, mince et nu, / Et simule l'amour en un lent frisson amer." (The speaker's use of the second person "toi" in referring to herself reinforces the idea of a de-centered subjectivity.) The final union between the speaker and her double, which bespeaks "the unbounded self love" (141) of the child's primary narcissism, is only a "simulation" of love, a counterfeit, since the love object is itself only an image. In addition, this final coupling (of the final couplet) is at once onanistic and necrophilic since the subject "loves" her "dead" self.

The "lent frisson amer" which ends the poem seems somehow to connote death, as though the integration of the self and her double somehow entails its destruction. There is something peculiarly Lacanian about this. While Freud's theory of the uncanny cannot adequately explain Hébert's negative presentation of what could potentially have been a healthful consolidation of a splintered subjectivity, the Lacanian concept of "extimacy (*l'extimité*) provides a clue.[3] Lacan generalizes Freud's notion of repression; rather than the interiorization of particular childhood complexes (castration complex, womb envy, repetition compulsion – which, not incidentally, were conceived principally with the male subject in mind) Lacan's version of the uncanny involves the reemergence of that state of being which existed prior to the formation of the ego during the "mirror stage." As Lacan explains in "The Mirror Stage as Formative of the Function of the I," it is only when the subject recognizes her double in the mirror as exactly that, her double, that she can possess an ego at all: "This form [the I in the mirror] situates the agency of the ego, before its social determination which will remain irreducible for the individual alone" (2). In this formulation, identity depends on the ability to recognize oneself. But since one cannot simultaneously recognize oneself and "be one" with oneself, identity involves – requires – a "lack," the essential bifurcation of the self. The uncanny thus presents itself as the removal of the "lack," a demonic parody of "finding yourself." Because this "self" exists prior to the establishment of the essential binary opposition separating subject from object, explains Mladen Dolar, "we can speak of the emergence of something that shatters well-known divisions and which cannot be situated within them" (6). Thus, for Lacan, it is not the threat of being replaced by one's double that fosters the feeling of the uncanny, but the possibility of *joining* with the double and thereby losing the ability to think of oneself as a subject any longer.

In "Vie de château," the reader is presented with precisely this crisis: the speaker would like to treat her mirror reflection as merely an object, a sign that, while relating to herself, is not herself. Unfortunately, the object refuses to respect that distinction; it binds itself to her. On one hand, this represents the recuperation of some part of herself that had been lost, for all intents and purposes "dead," but on the other, it is a gift that can only be accepted at the cost of giving up her life: "the lost part destroys reality instead of completing it" (Dolar 13). Consequently, I must take issue with Lorraine Weir who in her essay "'Fauna of Mirrors': the Poetry of Atwood and Hébert" asserts, "In the kingdom of mirrors, there is neither self nor the comforts of reliable mimesis" (104). On the contrary, the problem would seem to be one of *too much self*, a difficulty the mirrors reflect all too clearly. Thus the struggle here is not between the speaker and death (nor, by extension, the various forces which death is said to symbolize) but between the speaker and her own self. Death appears, paradoxically, as the spoils of victory, the self's successful annexation of its "other half."

A few questions naturally arise at this point: what kind of victory is this, and to whom does it belong, the speaker or her double? An exploration of these questions helps clarify the basic disagreements which frame the criticism of *Le Tombeau des rois*. While the speaker of "Vie de château" is clearly the victim of her double,

Hébert, in the final poem of the collection, turns this process on its head. Her speaker consciously seeks out her "dead" self (selves), and deploys the uncanny in a disruptive manner, *using* it as a means of addressing, if not undoing, those binary structures in which woman is subordinated. Hébert's poetry is therefore exceedingly political, but not in cultural nationalist terms, as some critics have proposed. It is political to the extent that it interrogates, and possibly subverts, the ideational and social formations underpinning traditional (patriarchal) epistemology, and problematizes the status of the subject within those formations.

As Monique Wittig points out in her collection of essays *The Straight Mind*, "Man and Woman . . . are political concepts of opposition" (29) which derive from the basic subject/object opposition that underlies all western epistemology, and from which the related construct of "public versus private" is likewise derived. The objectification of woman thus entails her relegation to the private sphere where she is denied status as a speaking subject, and where she is acted upon, rather than acts. "Radical speech," therefore, is for Wittig that which produces "a political transformation of the key concepts" (30) that underpin the subjection of women. Since the uncanny manifests itself as that which confuses categories of being, which blurs the line between subject and object, it therefore has the potential of becoming the site where radical speech is made possible.

There is an aspect of Freud's uncanny which is particularly suited to the question of the public/private dichotomy, and hence to the role of the uncanny within feminist poetics. It appears among the etymological extracts with which Freud begins his essay. He approaches the subject of the *"Unheimlich"* from its root-word and antonym, *"heimlich"* or *"heimisch,"* "meaning 'familiar'; 'native', 'belonging to the home'" (124). Of great interest to Freud is the fact that among the many meanings of *heimlich*, "it exhibits one which is identical with its opposite" (129):

> From the idea of "homelike", "belonging to the house", the further idea is developed of something withdrawn from the eyes of others, something concealed, secret, and this idea is expanded in many ways. (130)

By metamorphosing into its opposite, and so coming to mean both "familiar" and "secret," the etymology of *"heimlich"* itself mimics the mechanism of repression whereby what had once been familiar reappears as something mysterious and terrifying. "The *unheimlich* is what was once *heimisch,* home-like, familiar; the prefix "un" is the token of repression" (153). Freud fails to elaborate upon the role of the home within this dynamic; his interest lies in the adjectives, not the nouns.[4] However, the idea "belonging to the home" buried within the very name of the uncanny legitimizes some consideration of the role that domesticity – a category clearly fraught with contradiction – might play in the uncanny, especially in relation to a specifically female consciousness.

Since, as Weir notes, Hébert's speaker is "committed to the vocabulary of domestic order" (102), it is not surprising that the home presents itself as the principal locus of the uncanny in *Le Tombeau des rois*.

This is clearly revealed in "Vie de château" whose ironic title reflects the extent to which domesticity, and its implied anonymity and loneliness, is a sort of "living-death" for the speaker. Hébert develops this theme in an equally spooky poem entitled "La petite morte":

Une petite morte
s'est couchée en travers de la porte.

Nous l'avons trouvée au matin, abattue sur notre seuil
Come un arbre de fougère plein de gel. (53)

That the corpse is both feminine and small suggests its affinity with the mirror-corpse of "Vie de Château," representing the lost child-self of the speaker. In this case, however, the death of the child is directly related to a life of domestic boredom. Having fallen across the speaker's doorstep, the dead child prevents her from leaving the house. Trapped, she busies herself with house-work:

Nous nous efforçons de vivre à l'intérieur
Sans faire de bruit
Balayer la chambre
Et ranger l'ennui . . .

The speaker's use of the plural pronoun "nous" is significant in that it reflects a desire to speak for "woman" collectively about their collective experience of "une vie si minuscule et tranquille" (53).

But whereas the speaker of "Vie de château" resists her mirror double, that of "Une petite morte" wishes she could "dépasse l'envers de ce miroir limpide / Où cette soeur que nous avons / Se baigne bleu sous la lune." The mirror is both a way in (to a fuller self-consciousness) and out (beyond the threshold, into the public world). As Lacan suggests, it also assures the speaker's self-destruction: beyond the mirror is death; the "sister" she would join is a rotting corpse whose "odeur capiteuse" grows stronger. She does not, therefore, cross over, though she is tempted. Pierre-Hervé Lemieux writes:

> Tout cela fait que le *je* s'est approché le plus possible de l'état de la *petite morte*, allant aussi loin qu'un reste de vie le permet, frôlant la mort et rendu aux limites d'une vie qui s'epuise et se *minisculise* à mesure. La distance qui sépare la *soeur morte* et le *je* vivant a été reduite au minimum. Un pas de plus et elle est abolie, ce sera l'identification. (Lemieux 1978, 143)

It is not difficult to explain the speaker's temptation towards an identification with the "la petite morte" (at which point, thinking of Freud, symbol and symbolized merge) and to the abolition of her self: the "deep" mirrors of the uncanny provide a means of escape from the cloying confines of the home where she is not quite herself, not quite the speaking subject, not quite alive. Strangely, it is "normal," everyday existence that manifests itself as truly uncanny in *Le Tombeau des rois*. Precisely because the speaker is, emotionally and symbolically at least, *already* dead that she (a) can and (b) must precipitate what Slavoj Zizek calls the "second death," "the radical annihilation of the symbolic texture through which the so-called reality is constituted" (132). Paradoxically, only by "giving birth" to her (second) death can the speaker hope to achieve a life worth living.

Though the second death is, for Zizek, the most intense expression of the condition of extimacy, and naturally destructive to the subject, it is desperately embraced by the speaker in the final poem "Le Tombeau des rois." She has little choice – and nothing to lose. In an earlier poem, "Nuit," the speaker had claimed, "je ne déchiffre aucun mystère" (22). As a whole, *Le Tombeau des rois* can be understood as a movement toward the decoding of a mystery whose secret, once laid bare, must be embraced by the speaker. True to its elaboration of the search for identity through quest is the final poem's invocation of the myth of Theseus and the image of the labyrinth: "Quel fil d'Ariane me mène / Au long des dédales sourdes" (70). In the classical myth Theseus makes his way through the Cretan labyrinth trailing behind him a thread given to him by Ariadne. At the centre of the structure he encounters the Minotaur whom he fights and kills. Victorious, he follows the thread back to Ariadne, his love, who waits for him at the entrance grasping the thread's other end. In "Le Tombeau des rois," the reader is likewise presented with the archetypal labyrinth, and its confusing and disorienting effect is well-established by the eerie silence and gloomy half-light that pervades the poem's other images. But unlike Theseus, the speaker is not a male hero in search of a love object, but a female quester in search of self-knowledge. Nor does she follow the thread out of the labyrinth, but deeper into it and toward the final "confrontation by the self of those elements which had been feared or repressed" (Russell 44). And while the male hero's experience centres on trial and conquest, the dispatching of an enemy, that of the female speaker centres on sacrifice and surrender. She must become a "offrande rituelle et soumise" (71). These differences owe in part to Hébert's self-conscious refusal to repeat the patterns of patriarchal myth, but, also because the quest motif here is a version of the death drive, the speaker seeking her "second death" and the abolition of an undesirable reality.

Consequently, the setting is no less Freudian than mythic: the speaker descends "Vers les tombeaux des rois" in whose "chambres secrètes et rondes" she sacrifices her flesh to "le désir des gisants" who, she admits, "me couchent et me boivent" (72). Imagined as a sexual encounter (as in "Vie de château"), the speaker's fraternization with the dead approximates a renewal. Entering their chamber, she is "Étonnée / A peine née." "Scarcely born," the speaker is given license to dismantle the dream in which "cette enfant [est] liée par la cheville / Pareille à une esclave fascinée."[5] Significantly, Hébert places this nightmare of imprisonment in parentheses; it no longer applies, was displaced the moment the speaker began her descent toward the "tomb of the kings."

Her "sustained adventure" (as Russell calls it) in the kingdom of the dead thus follows the inexorable, if ironic, logic of the uncanny. The speaker first experiences a bifurcation of self; a recognition of the "lack;" she carries her heart on her fist "comme un faucon aveugle." The removal and exteriorization of her heart, traditionally symbolic of human essence, and its placement upon her fist – a gesture, simultaneously, of distancing, defiance, and declaration – parallels an encounter with the double since, as Mladen Dolar writes, the mirror image (like the poetic "heart") "is more fundamental than its owner: it institutes his substance, his essential being, his 'soul'" (12). Once the lack has been recognized, the speaker's reality loses its coherence. She, herself, loses (or abandons) control and is no longer "l'auteur du songe." A storm is building, "Déjà l'odeur bouge en des orages gonflés," as the speaker blindly advances toward a cataclysmic final encounter with the "sept grands pharaons d'ebene" who are roused from their coffins by "un frisson long."

The reappearance, in "Le Tombeau des rois," of the words "odeur" and "frisson" draws attention to the relationship between it and the earlier poems in which those terms played such key roles. The consciousness of this effect is confirmed by the following lines:

Ce n'est que la *profondeur de la mort* qui persiste,
Simulant le dernier tourment
Cherchant son apaisement
Et son éternité . . . (72, my italics)

"Le Tombeau des rois" completes the process begun in "Vie de château" and "La petite morte." Whereas the first evoked and invoked the uncanny, and the second related it to the potential subversion of the cultural codes that handicap female subjectivity, the last poem of the collection represents the final, necessary step toward the speaker's total affirmation of the self. That her "eternal appeasement" should take the form of a "final torment" is what marks her quest as uncanny.

This explains, in part at least, why the poem's final stanza has been regularly misinterpreted as *either* the speaker's victory *or* her defeat. Looked at from the point of view of the uncanny, such quibbling is rendered spurious. By definition, the uncanny is an affective mode which renders impossible such either/or distinctions. And since the conflict is within and between herself, rather than with sinister external forces *per se*, questions of defeat or triumph are moot. Either way she wins, but always at a tremendous cost. Failure to integrate with her double, her dead self, leaves her trapped in domesticity, "arranging *ennui*," yet success in this respect ensures her destruction because existence cannot tolerate a "lack of the lack."

The 'both/and-yet-neither/nor' character of this resolution is conveyed by the contradictions that dominate the final stanza of "Le Tombeau des rois." The speaker has been freed, "les morts . . .assassinés," her "membres dénoués," and a new dawn is breaking. However, she remains buried with the kings; the dawn is not directly experienced; it is only a "reflection" ["reflet"] that has "mislaid itself" ["s'égare"] in the tomb. She has already "sacrificed her flesh" in the name of the "songe horrible" of full consciousness. Tellingly, the eyes of the falcon which represents her heart are "crevées," though directed at the sunrise. The speaker knows too much, and must now reside in the realm she had only previously visited. Hébert's presentation of this sacrifice, and the speaker's apparent endorsement of its ironic salvation represents a pyrrhic victory. It is her condemnation of a world in which women suffer incompleteness, while men would seem to "lack" in plenitude. [6]

NOTES

1. Emile Talbot, for example, in his feminist reading of *Le Tombeau des rois* ("Anne Hébert's "La fille maigre": Gendering Poetics"), claims that the volume can be understood as a "radical affirmation of womanhood" (88) in a "Quebec still dominated by a centuries-old . . . discourse of abnegation" (91). Since *Le Tombeau des rois* works toward displacing this discourse, he holds that the volume as a whole "record[s] a victory over death," and the title poem itself provides a "liberating closure" (89). Likewise, Pierre-Hervé Lemieux – who suggests that the volume engages with the "master-images" that "had so long dominated the colonized, clericalized minds of the Québécois" – sees the collection as one in which "harsh revolt is given a highly personal expression and an ultimately liberating outcome" (1983, 342). Along these same lines, Susan Rosenstreich reads the poem as one "which reveals and challenges the subtle control the past exercises over the destinies of cultures" (65). She too celebrates the poem's "elaborated reality" and "poignant realism" (66). Without denying the text's historical and cultural specificity, or its obvious engagement with threatening social or ideological forces, I would like to counter the assumption that the poem's political potency must be predicated on a realistic or mimetic modality. In so doing, I also bear in mind Northrop Frye's observation (and warning) that "genuine allegory is a structural element in literature . . . and cannot be added by critical interpretation alone" (*Anatomy* 54).

2. What happens in the case of the double is that the subject can no longer think of himself as such, since mature self-understanding necessitates a belief in his singularity and uniqueness, no less than his coherence. Freud mentions another important means of evoking the uncanny, namely a loss of vision, or an attack upon the eyes. Though he ultimately reduces this fear to its psychological counterpart, the fear of castration, one can see here another version of dismemberment, but also, since the eyes are "windows to the soul," a fear of losing one's essential selfhood.

3. This neologism of Lacan's, used to express an awareness of the foreign, the alien within the intimate, is mentioned only a few times throughout the Seminars. However, it has been treated more rigorously in the work of Jacques-Alain Miller (see "Extimité" in *Lacanian Theory of Discourse: Subject, Structure, and Society* ed. Mark Bracher et al.), Slavoj Zizek (*The Sublime Object of Ideology*, especially chapter 4), and Mladen Dolar, whose essay "'I Shall be With You on Your Wedding Night': Lacan and the Uncanny" first introduced me to the concept. I might also add that an appeal to Lacan in the context of the uncanny has the added advantage of providing a means of circumventing the problem of the castration complex in dealing with the uncanny insofar as it relates to the psychology of women. As Ellen Peel writes in "Psychoanalysis and the Uncanny": "Regardless of uncanniness or literature, the very nature of some of the infantile complexes is questionable. A notorious example is Freud's inability to cope with the psychology of women. Even on the limp assumption women have castration complexes, those complexes must still be very different from those of people who do have penises. And if the reappearance of the castration complex seems uncanny to men, then it must be uncanny in a different way to women" (412).

4. This is somewhat surprising given that the house would seem to provide an excellent metaphor for a conscious that contains and hides the "secret" life of the unconscious. One might surmise that Freud did not avail himself of this rhetorical opportunity because the "home" is already gendered female, whereas the uncanny subject is male in every case.

5. There may be an allusion here to Oedipus whose ankles were similarly bound. The child in this case is clearly female, however, but she, too, is imprisoned no less than Oedipus, whose destiny was inescapable. Whether the speaker's life is similarly tragic remains to be seen.

6. Thanks to Ray Ellenwood for his helpful commentary on an earlier version of this essay.

WORKS CITED

Miller, Jacques-Alain. "Extimité." *Lacanian Theory of Discourse: Subject, Structure, and Society*. Ed. Mark Bracher et al. New York: New York UP, 1994. 74-87.

Dolar, Mladen. "'I Shall be with You on Your Wedding-Night': Lacan and the Uncanny." *October* 58 (Fall 1991): 5-23.

Freud, Sigmund. "The Uncanny." *On Creativity and the Unconscious: Papers on the Psychology of Art, Literature, Love, Religion*. New York: Harper, 1958. 122-161.

Frye, Northrop. *Anatomy of Criticism: Four Essays*.

Hébert, Anne. *Le Tombeau des rois*. Québec: Institut Littéraire du Québec, 1953.

Lacan, Jacques. "The Mirror Stage as Formative of the Fuction of the I." *Écrits: A Selection*. Trans. Alan Sheridan. New York: Norton, 1977.

Lemieux, Pierre-Hervé. "Anne Hébert." *The Oxford Companion to Canadian Literature*. Toronto: Oxford UP, 1983.

——. *Entre songe et parole: Structure du* Tombeau des Rois *d'Anne Hébert*. Ottawa: Ottawa UP, 1978.

Peel, Ellen. "Psychoanalysis and the Uncanny." *Comparative Literature Studies* 17.4 (December 1980): 410-417.

Rosenstreich, Susan L. "Counter-Traditions: The Marginal Poetics of Anne Hébert."

Traditionalism, Nationalism, and Feminism: Women Writers of Quebec. Eds. Paula Gilbert Lewis and Elaine Marks. Lewis-Paula-Gilbert. Westport: Greenwood, 1985. 63-70.

Russell, Delbert W. *Anne Hébert.* Boston: Twayne, 1983.

Talbot, Émile J. "Anne Hébert's 'La fille maigre': Gendering Poetics." *Studies in Canadian Literature* 20.1 (Summer 1995): 80-92.

Weir, Lorraine. "'Fauna of Mirrors': The Poetry of Hébert and Atwood." *Ariel* 10.3 (1979): 99-113.

Wittig, Monique. *The Straight Mind.* Boston: Beacon, 1992.

Zizek, Slavoj. *The Sublime Object of Ideology.* London: Verso, 1989.

Zukofsky, Louis. "Anew #10." *Complete Short Poetry.* Baltimore: Johns Hopkins UP, 1991. 81.

Re-Writing Women's Destinies in Anne Hébert's *La Cage* and *L'Île de la Demoiselle*

ELODIE ROUSSELOT

Anne Hébert's literary oeuvre shows a recurrent concern with Quebec's past and the lives of some of its long forgotten female characters. This interest is evident in such works as *Kamouraska* and *Le premier jardin* where the author focuses on the tragic life-stories of actual Quebecois women, in what becomes an attempt to "re-write" Quebecois history. This interest is also visible in two plays which have received relatively little critical attention: *La Cage* and *L'Île de la Demoiselle*, published jointly in 1990. This essay will show in what ways both plays illustrate Anne Hébert's effort to re-interpret Quebec's past, and to create a specifically female historical space in which oppressed female figures are given an opportunity to make themselves heard and to control their destinies.

La Cage draws its inspiration from an actual incident which took place in 1763, shortly after the British conquest of *Nouvelle France*. It revolves around Marie-Josephte Corriveau, a widow convicted at the age of thirty by a British military court for the murder of her second husband. In conformity with English law, Marie-Josephte Corriveau was con-

39

demned to death by hanging and to having her body exposed in an iron cage "indefinitely," as a way to make an example of her. However, the local population pleaded to have her body removed, and after forty days on display she was finally buried. Her story came up again almost a century later, when a cage containing human remains was dug up from a local cemetery, and was assumed to have been hers.[1] The particularly shocking and exceptional punishment of having a criminal's dead body exposed and buried in an iron cage deeply marked the local popular imagination and gave rise to all sorts of legends and myths surrounding the character of *la Corriveau*. She has since become an integral part of the history and popular folklore of Quebec, and her story has inspired many Quebecois artists. Moreover, like "much of Quebec's newly reinterpreted past," *la Corriveau* emerged in the 1960s from "the depths of Quebec's history of oppression to become the symbol of a people victimized and imprisoned within an alien culture" (Green 102). She became both a figure of feminist rehabilitation and the incarnation of the nationalist plight, a "folk heroine, capable of representing Quebec to the outside world" (Green 101-2). This essay proposes to examine Anne Hébert's re-interpretation of the story of *la Corriveau*, and to focus in particular on her use of the fairy tale form as a means of raising questions regarding the authority of historical writing. The link between the female protagonist and the natural world, as well as the play's representation of marriage as a source of imprisonment for women, will also be addressed.

The second part of this essay will focus on *L'Île de la Demoiselle*, set in 1540 Canada and based on the true story of Marguerite de Nontron, a young French noblewoman sent into exile with her maid and her lover on the deserted *île des Démons*, in the estuary of the St. Lawrence. Marguerite de Nontron was part of an expedition bound for Canada and led by Captain Jean-François La Roque de Roberval, her guardian, who pronounced the deportation sentence against her for reasons of "immodest" behaviour. The purpose of the expedition was to found a French colony on the new continent, but the mission failed, and after a particularly harsh winter Roberval and the rest of the colonists all returned to France. The conditions of life on the *île des Démons* were also extremely challenging and claimed the lives of Marguerite's lover, their baby, and her maid; only Marguerite remained alive. She was eventually discovered and rescued twenty-nine months later by fishermen from Brittany who took her back to France.[2] This historical anecdote was first told by Marguerite de Navarre in her *Heptaméron*, and has inspired several creative re-writings since. In the present study of *L'Île de la Demoiselle*, we will reveal another attempt on Hébert's part to re-interpret the life-story of a victimised female figure from Quebec's past, while focussing especially on the patriarchal social structure of the time, on the important role the wilderness plays in the heroine's exile, and on the sense of empowerment and liberation she eventually gains from her ordeal.

In *La Cage*, Ludivine Corriveau is unhappily married to cruel Elzéar, whose passion for hunting is contrasted to her more benevolent attitude towards Nature. Ludivine suffers from a curse cast upon her at birth by "Black Fairies," who declared her unable to have children; however, her sterility is counter-balanced by the charitable and nurturing nature of her character: she acts as a sort of "Earth Mother" figure who does good in the local community and offers food and shelter to those in need. The play reaches a tragic climax when, one night, Elzéar returns home unexpectedly from a several year long hunting trip. He frightens Ludivine into thinking she is being attacked, and she shoots him with the hunting gun he had left for her protection. She realises too late her mistake, and Elzéar dies of his gunshot wound. Ludivine is subsequently accused of murder by Judge John Crebessa, an English magistrate recently settled in Canada, who sees in her action a plot to get rid of her husband. She is given a clearly unfair trial, where it is obvious from the start that her sentence has been pre-decided: Judge Crebessa is intent on getting her hanged, and on having her body exposed in an iron cage. As he is about to read the verdict, however, he suffers a sudden death caused by the inability of his "dark nature" to cope with the love expressed by Ludivine's *protégés* for her. Quite figuratively and literally, therefore, it seems Crebessa dies of a "heart attack." Ludivine is then free to go, as is John Crebessa's wife, Rosalinde, and the play ends on a happy scene of celebration.

The play's structure is very similar to that of a fairy tale; this is visible for instance in the list of characters, which includes a "wicked step-family," seven "White Fairies," seven "Black Fairies," and the "seven Deadly

Sins," who are real protagonists in the story and appear at Ludivine's trial. The recurrence of the number seven, the symbolism of the colours black and white, as well as the actual nature of these characters, all seem to locate the play within the genre of the fairy tale, as does the fact that these characters are fundamentally divided along the lines of good and bad, or victims and persecutors. In the play, the former are rewarded with freedom, love and happiness, while the latter are punished with death. The story's happy ending featuring the young lover (Hyacinthe) reunited with his beloved (Ludivine), and the rich heiress (Rosalinde) delivered from the malevolent brute holding her prisoner (John Crebessa), is yet again in keeping with fairy tale conventions. For that reason, Grazia Merler notices that the play revolves around a simple, but subversive, intrigue where tragedy is transformed into fairy tale (188), while Micheline Cambron points out that the narrative technique of the tale, and the refusal to follow the narrative order dictated by historiography, are highlighted in Hébert's play (201).

The fact however that *La cage* draws on both religious and fairy tale symbols, as in "Fairies" paired up with "Deadly Sins", seems to bring about a criticism of the puritanical religious beliefs of John Crebessa and of Ludivine's fellow villagers, visible in the play through their intolerance and narrow-mindedness. This association of religion with myth is noticeable also in the opening of the play, which describes the birth scenes of Ludivine and Rosalinde, on each side of the Atlantic Ocean, and each attended by White and Black Fairies. In a story line reminiscent of *Sleeping*

Beauty, where fairy godmothers offer gifts and make predictions about the newborn baby princess, Ludivine and Rosalinde receive the like from the White, or "good" Fairies, and the Black, or "wicked" Fairies. The religious element comes, however, from the fact that these birth scenes are described in the stage directions as a "[c]rèche vivante à droite, crèche vivante à gauche" (Hébert 1990, 16) [nativity scene on the left, nativity scene on the right].[3] As the Fairies bring their gifts, the parents are kneeling over each baby resting on the ground before them. The scenes are thus deeply evocative of the birth of Jesus, and the Fairies do remind one of the visit of the three Kings. Merler notes that the Fairies parody the birth of Christ, as is suggested by the indication that they are "lourdes d'étranges merveilles cachées [. . .] . Nous cherchons deux enfants nouveau-nés. L'étoile qui nous guida [. . .] s'est éteinte soudain" (1992, 189 quoting from Hébert 1990, 13) [heavy with strange and hidden marvels [. . .]. We are looking for two newborn babies. The star guiding us [. . .] has suddenly disappeared]. Hébert's play thus creates a parallel between Judeo-Christian myths and fairy tale conventions, subverting in the process the holiness of the beliefs the religious myths have given birth to. By drawing links between fairy tales and religion, Hébert also demonstrates the similarities of symbols and systems of belief between both. She performs an interesting gender transformation by presenting us with what could be seen as two female Christs, who will be persecuted by the puritan society of their time and become martyrs to the cause of women's freedom. This, once again, seems to highlight Hébert's attempt at undermining the authority of the religious ideology which has played a part in women's social oppression in the past.

Another important element of the fairy tale genre is the figure of the witch, present in the play through the characters of the Black Fairies. The heroine, on the other hand, is benevolent and charitable, but does not indulge in any witchcraft activities. The point is important to make as *la Corriveau*, as she has inhabited Quebecois oral and written folkloric tradition over the past 240 years, has often been described as a witch.[4] The symbol of the witch also became recurrent in the work of Quebecois women writers during the 1970s: in an attempt to define tropes and values proper to women, these writers sought to create "a complex figure, at once symbolic and real, historical and metaphorical." In this process, many wrote about "Quebec's own native witch," *la Corriveau* (Saint-Martin 1991, 67).[5] But Mary Jean Green observes that Marie-Josephte Corriveau was "transformed" into a witch by her fellow Quebecois: she was condemned solely for murder, but the shocking and exceptional character of her punishment, as well as rumours that she might have killed her first husband too, struck the popular imagination and gave rise to all sorts of superstitious speculation. Green talks of the double oppression, or "double colonisation," suffered by *la Corriveau*: although "it is a foreign conqueror that hanged her as a murderess, it is the patriarchal discourse of her own society that condemned her as a witch" (2001, 102), the progression from murderess to witch being "almost inevitable, for witchcraft is the ultimate crime with which women have traditionally been charged, both in history and in fairy tales" (2001, 101). Green adds that contemporary re-examination of witchcraft accusations has shown that they were often a way of condemning social marginality and punishing female deviance (2001, 101).

Hébert's play seems to show an understanding of this in its representation of a central protagonist who is fundamentally good, but vilified by both the foreign authorities and her fellow villagers. Judge John Crebessa suspects Ludivine of adultery and pronounces her guilty before her trial has even begun, while Elzéar's in-laws, the "wicked step-family" of the story, declare that "[l]a débauche la plus infâme, l'orgie, le sabbat, toutes les cochoncetés de la terre se donnaient rendez-vous dans la cabane de Ludivine Corriveau" (Hébert 1990, 93-4) [the most infamous debauchery, orgy, Sabbath, and all the world's obscenities would meet in Ludivine Corriveau's shack]. Hébert shows the motif of witchcraft, or evil doings, emerging in the testimony of Ludivine's fellow Quebecois, as it did in the case of Marie-Josephte. She highlights the cruel and prejudiced process by which a woman accused of murder is demonised by her society; in this particular instance, Hébert reveals not only the role played by the foreign conqueror, but also that played by Quebec itself in the victimisation of some of its own citizens. Therefore, by telling her own version of the story of *la Corriveau*, Hébert re-writes this particular aspect of Quebecois popular history and addresses the problematic role played by the foreign conqueror, as well as the gender-biased representations of women by coloniser and colonised alike. Through her focus on this historical incident, and her choice to turn it into a piece of literature, Hébert is able to valorise the story of *la Corriveau*, and to figuratively repair the wrongs done to her in the past.

Regarding the play's protagonists and their relation to historical accuracy, Judge John Crebessa is an interesting character: he is not an actual historical character, but yet he is historical in so far as Hébert's work is concerned. Judge John Crebessa is indeed briefly referred to on two occasions in Hébert's 1970 novel *Kamouraska*, where he becomes the symbol of the heroine's paranoid fear that the authorities are trying to catch her compromising her hard-earned appearance of innocence. In *La cage*, Judge John Crebessa plays a much more central role: he is the chief agent of persecution of Ludivine, and is described as a dark character motivated by malevolent purposes. His malice is played out on two different levels: the bias and superiority he shows towards the local Quebecois people, which seems to be linked to the fact that he is from England, and the misogyny he shows towards Ludivine and Rosalinde, his wife. One may find surprising, however, that a character who does not possess any actual historical existence should be mentioned twice, in two different literary works, twenty years apart from each other. The recurrence of the character's name, and the similarities in his role in each story, seem to highlight Hébert's wish to draw a link between both works, and to have Elisabeth d'Aulnières's story in *Kamouraska* and Ludivine Corriveau's in *La cage* read in light of each other. Beyond the resemblances between the two heroines' predicaments, as they both face the law and death penalty for the murder of an abusive husband, it seems Hébert is not only telling Elisabeth's and Ludivine's story, but also every woman's (her)story, regardless of the historical period in which she lives. Hébert thus does not simply re-write history but also transcends it by going beyond its temporal boundaries, and showing the presence of a fundamental link between oppressed women throughout time.

In this context, the use of the fairy tale form helps establish the idea of a tale incessantly repeating itself, and carrying truths, or values, relevant to any audience, regardless of their historical era. The fairy tale transcends the normal human boundaries of time and reality by featuring timeless and supernatural events, or characters. It also has implications in terms of a particular notion of historical narrative: indeed, the prominence of the Fairies in the play, and the way in which they dictate the future, seem to suggest that historical events are pre-determined, and that history is pre-ordered along criteria of birth, class and gender. However, the fact that the Fairies' predictions do not eventually come true highlights the importance of the role played by the heroine: she shows that by resisting this pre-determination, she is able to change a fate which, at first, seemed immutable. The fairy tale form thus becomes a crucial tool for Hébert in her denunciation of the relentless oppression women have suffered in the past, but also in her illustration of the fact that the course of history can be altered through opposing this oppression.

Furthermore, Nature and the free wilderness of the New World, two important themes in the play, are linked to an expression of gender. Male characters stand out by their dislike of Nature, or their persistent attempt at destroying it, as with Elzéar's passion for hunting. Female characters, on the other hand, and Ludivine in particular, are at ease and in harmony with Nature, and pay special attention to its rhythms and seasonal changes. In the context of a play emphasising the arrival of the coloniser from England to Canada (namely Judge John Crebessa and his wife Rosalinde), and symbolically describing the divide between the two continents, it seems imperative to link the treatment of the trope of Nature to that of the particularities attached to the wilderness of the New World, particularities which are lost upon the Eurocentric coloniser, but which are celebrated by the local female Quebecois folks.

John Crebessa is a good example of the coloniser's suspicions towards the New World: he forbids his wife Rosalinde to wander in the wilderness, for fear of the effects this might have on her, while he himself dislikes the countryside, which he perceives as a corrupting force needing to be tamed and controlled. Indeed, he describes his role as "gardien des moeurs de ce pays" (Hébert 1990, 97) [keeper of this country's morals], thus emphasising the link he sees between colonisation, taming Nature, and establishing civilisation, in the form of European-based social morals. However, the play highlights how Crebessa's civilising aims are destructive towards the harmoniously balanced realm of the natural world: the colonial intervention disrupts the natural order, which suggests that the coloniser is unfit to rule the land. Moreover, the divide between Old World and New World, coloniser and wilderness, is transcended in the play by the opposition between man and woman, as seen through the character of Rosalinde, who is British and a coloniser but ultimately a victim of her husband's cruel patriarchal authority. The analogy between colonial and patriarchal power seems to be reinforced through the choice of a common target for both: Nature, which is opposed to (colonial) civilisation, but equated to a source of freedom for the female characters. The obviously problematic association of the colonised land with the tamed female body is however resolved in Hébert's work through the suggestion that the wilderness ultimately wins over the patriarchal husband and male coloniser (both of whom die in the play), while offering a haven of peace and harmony to those who respect it. The traditional trope that possessing the land is similar to taking possession of a female body is therefore negated in the play through the successful resistance of both Nature and women.

Through her contact with the natural world, Ludivine becomes a nurturing figure and a source of life for those in need in the local community, a form of Quebecois Earth Mother: as Hyacinthe notices, Ludivine "rayonne partout" [exerts her influence everywhere] and "[t]out le paysage et tous ceux qui sont dans ce paysage, bêtes et gens, s'enchantent de vivre avec elle et par elle" (Hébert 1990, 108) [the entire landscape as well as those living in this landscape, animals and people, delight in living with her and through her]. Ludivine is thus instrumental in bringing and sustaining life, a quality which she was unable to enjoy in her infertile marriage to Elzéar. Annabelle M. Rea sees in Hébert's version of *la Corriveau*'s story a reinforcement of the author's "long-standing criticism of family structure in Quebec" (2001, 23). Rea explains that Hébert's treatment of the theme of family in the play is a powerful rejection of the official Quebecois ideology which glorified motherhood, and has historically encouraged women to have large families through the motif of the *revanche des berceaux*. For Rea, Ludivine's "adoptive family," in the sense of a "chosen" family, here composed of the excluded members of society, and most importantly her sterility, are ways to oppose this ideology (2001, 23-4). Ludivine therefore becomes a figure of resistance to the dominant ideology, and a source of inspiration for other Quebecois women. The challenging wilderness of the New World is therefore a source of inspiration for the oppressed female characters of *La cage*: the coloniser attempts to tame it, but eventually fails in his enterprise, the same way the male characters are unsuccessful in their efforts to control the female protagonists.

The play also features a strong criticism of marriage, which is represented as an abusive prison, a cage, like the one used to punish criminals in the story. The title of the play therefore refers to both the punishment received by *la Corriveau*, and, more generally, to women's imprisonment through matrimony. The metaphor is enacted on a very literal level, through the presence of two cages on stage, one on each side of the Atlantic Ocean and for each of the main female protagonists. Rosalinde's cage is golden, a *clin d'oeil* to the French expression "une cage dorée," often referring to a wealthy, but unhappy, union. In the scene where John and Rosalinde's wedding celebration takes place the golden cage is decorated with white ribbons and flowers, thus highlighting the parallels between marriage and prison, regardless of how pretty the cage may be. The scene ends with Rosalinde entering the cage and John locking her up and keeping the key, which comes to symbolise the instrument of the wife's persecution by her husband. Being the keeper of the key gives ultimate power to John over the destiny of his wife, and over that of Ludivine too, later on, when he attempts to pass a death sentence upon her and to have her body imprisoned in a cage. The key also seems to become the phallic symbol of John's sexual and authoritarian desire over these women's bodies: "j'affirmerai mes droits de maître et d'époux. [. . .] Que seule la clef de fer demeure intacte, reconnaissable entre toutes, dans ma main" (Hébert 1990, 36-7) [I'll assert my rights as master and husband. [. . .] May only the iron key remain intact, recognisable between all, in my hand]. The scene of John and Rosalinde's wedding does echo those suggestions of possession through violence, both physically and morally. The bride's loss of virginity in particular, which is associated with the loss of her (maiden) name, is described as a rather coercive act, as illustrated through the song of the guests' choir:

Couvre les cris de la mariée
Dans les bras de son époux
Au premier soir de ses noces. [...]
La mariée a perdu son nom et sa couronne,
Pour le meilleur et pour le pire,
Jusqu'à ce que mort s'ensuive,
Est devenue Lady John Crebessa. (Hébert 1990, 35-6)

[Cover the cries of the bride
In her groom's arms
On her first wedding night. [...]
The bride has lost her name and her garland,
For better and for worse,
Until death do them part,
Has become Lady John Crebessa.]

The grotesque discrepancy between the traditionally merry singing, typical of a wedding celebration, and the actual words of the guests' song somehow emphasises the bride's powerlessness, and the institutionalisation of her cruel predicament. Marriage is thus described as the tool of women's oppression, both physically, through the loss of virginity and the confinement to the home, a form of domestic "cage", and morally, through the loss of identity. In this context, the traditional wedding vow for husband and wife to remain together until "death do them part" becomes a sombre omen, laden with a sense of foreboding as to the ways in which women can set themselves free from the prison of matrimony. Ludivine's cage in the play is made of iron, and has black ravens resting on it, seemingly waiting for her body to be locked inside. Once again, the imagery of death and decay, through Crebessa's repetitive jubilations at the idea that the ravens will pick at Ludivine's eyeballs and at her dead body, helps emphasise the harsh treatment of the female protagonists by the male characters, and as a result reinforces the negative and destructive vision of marriage produced by the play. Consequently, the idea of husband murder out of self-defence and protection is clearly expressed: Ludivine admits during her trial, "[j]'ai voulu me protéger [. . .]. J'ai tiré, par peur, pour me défendre" (Hébert 1990, 102) [I tried to protect myself [. . .]. I shot out of fear, to defend myself].

A crucial aspect of the nature of Ludivine's – and Marie-Josephte's – punishment is that it came to symbolise the cruelty of the coloniser, the English "nouveaux maîtres," whose sentence was perceived as a symptom of their cultural difference, and would inspire and haunt Quebecois imagination for centuries to come. The practice of exposing a criminal's dead body in a cage "indefinitely" was totally unheard of and deeply shocking to the French Canadian population of the time. In England, however, this was a current legal practice, and remained so up until the nineteenth century (see Lacourcière 238). *La Corriveau*'s tragic fate thus became inextricably linked to an old British custom, and came to be seen as an expression of a foreign and potentially cruel power. Additionally, the fact that this punishment was only ever used on one other occasion throughout Canada's history, helps emphasise the extraordinary aspect of *la Corriveau*'s death, and possibly explains the numerous legends and superstitions her story gave rise to. It is important to note that Marie-Josephte Corriveau was tried by court martial: there is a sense that she was not given a fair trial because of this, and that the evidence under which she was convicted was "circumstantial at best" (Green 2001, 100). In Hébert's play, Ludivine is not tried by court martial, but her trial is clearly shown to be a parody of justice, as seen through the intervention of the seven Deadly Sins, which are "invités d'honneur [au] procès" (Hébert 1990, 94) [guests of honour at the trial], and which help highlight the oppressive religious and social prejudices set against Ludivine. Her sentence is also pronounced before her trial has even begun, an illustration perhaps of both the irregularity of the judicial proceedings involved, and of the ineluctability of her fate. Moreover, the trial is clearly defined in terms of British law, as seen in the reference to the "témoins de la Couronne" (Hébert 1990, 90) [Crown's witnesses]. Hébert's play does suggest that Ludivine is a victim of political, and more particularly colonial, circumstances, that she is unable to fully grasp the laws by which she is judged, and that, as a result, she cannot defend herself effectively.

It is still felt today that Marie-Josephte Corriveau's sentence was unfair and symptomatic of an attempt by the coloniser to gain control over the (recently) colonised French Canada. It seems the English authorities viewed *la Corriveau*'s crime as being particularly undermining to them, not only because it involved murder, but also because it was committed by a woman.[6] Maureen O'Meara observes that, perhaps, "the undermining of male authority in the families of the "Canadiens" was seen as destructive to the order of the colony by its new British masters" (2001, 176).

One can thus easily see why *la Corriveau* has become such a powerful symbol of the expression of the victimisation of Quebec by a foreign order. However, Anne Hébert's particular stance in her interpretation of *la Corriveau*'s story emphasises her choice to highlight the ways in which women were specifically affected by that foreign power, and, most importantly, the double persecution they suffered through the agency of their own patriarchal society.

L'Île de la Demoiselle reveals another attempt on the part of the author to re-interpret the life-story of a victimised female figure from the past. The play shows how, when Jean-François La Roque de Roberval's ships hit a terrible storm, the colonists feel the trip is cursed by a sin committed by someone on board. They direct their suspicion at Marguerite de Nontron, Roberval's ward, and discover, to Roberval's dismay, that Marguerite has fallen in love with one of the artisans on board. Roberval, who had unsuccessfully attempted to woo Marguerite previously, is infuriated by this insult, and punishes her by abandoning her with her maid and her lover on the *île des Démons*. Marguerite alone survives against all odds, and swears a bloody revenge on the person of Roberval. She suffers from delirium and has hallucinatory visions in which she sees him murdered. Sailors eventually find her two years and five months later, and tell her that Roberval has died in mysterious circumstances, with similar injuries to those Marguerite had wished upon him. Relieved at the news, she agrees to go back to France, and the sailors re-name the island "île de la Demoiselle" in her honour.

The play thus returns to the time when France carried out its very first colonial project in North America, and clearly sets up the political context of that period. It is interesting to note that the official intentions of the colonists – carry out the religious conversion of the "savages" and establish "une colonie très catholique" (Hébert 1990, 119) – are counter-balanced by unofficial reasons, motivated by the appeal of the "gold" and "diamonds" to be found in abundance in the New World, following from the sixteenth-century misconception that Canada is "un petit bout de l'Asie fabuleusement riche" (Hébert 1990, 123) [the little tip of fabulously wealthy Asia], and that spices "poussent dans la neige" (Hébert 1990, 124) [grow in the snow]. Therefore, under cover of religious zeal, the play illustrates the mercantile interest of the colonists and their Eurocentric prejudices: when speaking of the Natives, a nobleman declares "ils n'ont pas d'âme et il faudra les massacrer tous" (Hébert 1990, 123) [they have no soul and we will have to kill them all]. The play also reveals some of the political tensions surrounding Marguerite's punishment: Roberval is indeed said to be a former Protestant, who had been exiled for his faith, and allowed back in France by King François I upon condition that he converted to Catholicism. After doing so, he also had to comply with the King's request to take an expedition to Canada on a religious mission, "afin d'afficher sa conversion aux yeux de tous" (Hébert 1990, 122) [so as to flaunt his conversion for all to see]. However, when the storm hits the ships, and rumours start spreading that the expedition is cursed, Roberval is only too keen to find another culprit to divert suspicion from him. Marguerite's illegitimate love affair provides such a diversion, and Roberval thus has both personal and political reasons for punishing her, and for making an example of that punishment. She therefore pays the price of her liberty not only for falling in love with a man below her station, but also to save the Captain's honour.

The first part of the play, set on board the ships, thus shows the unfair victimisation of the heroine, and in what ways the society of the time was corrupted by hypocrisy and greed, as condoned by the Church. D.W. Russell observes that in that society, women's behaviour is dictated by the patriarchy which, in the person of Captain Roberval, is "maître à bord, après Dieu" (1982, 176 quoting from Hébert 1990, 137) [master on board, after God]. Captain Roberval is indeed not only responsible for finding a suitable match for Marguerite (which he covets for himself), but also for administrating her land and fortune. Wangari Wa Nyatetu-Waigwa sees in the coloniser's desire "to reserve Marguerite for himself" the fact that "in a sense, she mirrors the supposedly uninhabited land he is going to settle in Canada" (190). Through the figure of Roberval, therefore, we are presented with an oppressive view of men's power, a power which carries ultimate authority over women. When the heroine fails to respect that authority, Roberval pronounces a death sentence against her by deporting her to the desert-like *île des Démons*. In this regard, Roberval is very similar to Judge Crebessa in *La cage*, and becomes a symbol of women's persecution and patriarchal domination. Mélissa McKay notices that in *L'Île de la Demoiselle* the heroine is not only imprisoned figuratively in the society in which she lives, but she is also literally locked up on several occasions. McKay points to the recurrent imagery of imprisonment, confinement and exile in the play, as when Marguerite is abandoned on the desert island, but also during the trip, where she is confined to her cabin in the ship's hold, and through the references to her childhood, spent in a convent (24-5). Once again, such imagery is also present in *La cage* and helps emphasise the subservience of women's social status. It is interesting to note, however, that *L'Île de la Demoiselle* offers a rather positive vision of marriage, and not that of a prison-like "cage," as found in *La cage*, through the fact that Marguerite and Nicolas fall in love and freely choose each other. Nevertheless, their union is not sealed by any "official" or religious ceremony, but based solely on their mutual agreement and understanding.

In the second part of the play, set on the *île des Démons*, the wilderness provides a space in which the heroine can be liberated from the dictates of civilisation, and more particularly, from those of patriarchy. Marguerite is indeed seen to progressively lose her "conditioning" as a young noblewoman, and to become more and more "animalised" through her contact with the wilderness. The arrival on the island is described in terms of a new beginning by the heroine, who questions the relevance of the social class system by taking for "husband" a man below her station, and by advocating equality of class between her and her maid. The wilderness offers a place where the heroine can create a new society of equals: "[c]ette île est un pays sans Seigneur ni Dame, tous égaux" (Hébert 1990, 204) [this island is a country with no Lord nor Lady, all equals], while she tells her unborn child: "tu naîtras libre et jamais M. de Roberval ou quelque autre puissance de ce monde n'aura de pouvoir sur toi" (Hébert 1990, 204) [you will be born free and never will M. de Roberval or any other powers of this world have control over you]. Marguerite thus embraces the potential for change available in the New World of the island, and in particular the increased freedom of a society rid of patriarchy. As a result, she progressively abandons her feminine proper behaviour, as taught to her by the nuns at the convent, and adopts a de-gendered attitude: "je porterai le pantalon de Nicolas pour être plus à l'aise, dans mon île" (Hébert 1990, 237) [I will wear Nicolas's trousers to be more at ease on my island]. The island thus provides a locus where traditional class and gender boundaries are broken and re-defined by the heroine. It is also where she sets about planting a garden, composed of wheat, buckwheat and oats, and tells Nicolas:

Ce rang de blé-là sera sacré et il poussera des enfants comme les coquelicots mêlés au blé. Nous peuplerons toute l'Île. (Hébert 1990, 207)

[This row of wheat will be sacred and children will grow like poppies mingled with wheat. We will populate the whole island.]

The idea of planting a garden, and the reference to wheat in particular, remind one of Hébert's novel *Le premier jardin*, which describes how Louis Hébert and Marie Rollet, Hébert's ancestors, were the first colonists to plant a garden in the New World, and how they harvested the first sheaf of wheat. The idea of a "first garden" suggests also, of course, the Garden of Eden; as Kelton W. Knight has pointed out, "Marguerite de Nontron becomes a metaphor of Canada's first mother, a primeval Eve who plants the New World's first Garden of Eden" (39). In this context, the fertility of the land is symbolically associated with that of the female body ("children mingled with wheat"), and both are linked in a harmonious way, as with Ludivine and the natural world of *La cage*.

However, as the conditions of life on the island prove harder for the deportees, the wilderness evolves from the benevolent and inviting setting evoked in *La cage*, to a rather threatening and potentially deadly world, giving rise to all sorts of scary hallucinations. In particular, the wild birds inhabiting the island become the source of obsessive fears for Marguerite and her maid, while Nicolas is eventually attacked and fatally wounded by one of them. Marguerite also has visions that her unborn child is developing monstrous features:

> Et si j'allais accoucher d'une créature pleine d'écailles et de plumes? Aïe mon enfant est un monstre. Il me mange le cœur. J'étouffe. Il nous dévorera tous, vous verrez. (Hébert 1990, 217)

[What if I gave birth to a creature covered in scales and feathers? Aïe my child is a monster. He is eating my heart. I'm choking. He will devour us all, you'll see.]

The image of the animalised child seems to indicate that the contact with the wilderness has strange effects on the female protagonist's vision of maternity, while she very clearly associates Nature with motherhood (once again, through the image of the "children mingled to wheat"). The fear of giving birth to monstrous children, which the female pioneer experiences, seems to locate the process of animalisation in that of maternity: as a result, Mother Nature and the female colonist are linked and likened to a distorted and potentially threatening vision of motherhood. Moreover, the island, at first the source of a new beginning, eventually becomes a hostile and sterile environment, causing death and preventing life from springing forth. Ultimately, after her companions and baby have died, Marguerite's fears turn into a rage for revenge, while she loses her civilised self and returns to a primal, animal state:

Mon pauvre Nicolas, ta belle et tendre amoureuse bascule parmi les harpies, perd toute face humaine et s'arme jusqu'aux dents, pour réclamer justice et réparation! (Hébert 1990, 229)

[My poor Nicolas, your beautiful and sweet lover turns into a harpy, loses all human appearance and arms herself to the teeth, to ask for justice and compensation!]

It is as though Marguerite needs to lose her human appearance in order to be empowered and to obtain revenge. Her femininity and social decorum have caused her previous powerlessness; only through this process of "animalisation" can she be liberated from a subservient female status. This loss of femininity becomes obvious when the heroine declares: "[j]e ne suis plus une femme, ni rien de convenable. Ce que je suis devenue n'a pas de nom en aucune langue connue" (Hébert 1990, 233) [I am no longer a woman nor anything proper. What I have become has no name in any known language]. The loss of properness, and in particular the inability to speak her state, indicate a total breakdown of civilisation and its values. In the play, in order to shed her social conditioning, Marguerite has to renounce language; she is then able to return to a primitive, animal state. Nyatetu-Waigwa observes that "[t]he heroine's journey, even when physical, often becomes a psychological struggle to reappropriate her space," where "[h]er self becomes the realm of contention to be wrested from the patriarchy." She adds that because of "its inner nature and because of the role played by physical space, this journey bears many similarities to liminality," for "[i]solation and stripping, characteristics of liminality, become also some of the major features of the heroine's journey towards repossession and redefinition of her self" (188). Therefore, exile provides the means for Marguerite to discard the oppressive values of her society, while the alienation it brings becomes a source of self-definition and empowerment.

This process is not carried out without a struggle however, but described in terms of a tension within Marguerite, between her resistance to the wilderness and her attraction to it. This tension is expressed through an imagined dialogue between the heroine and one of the nuns at her former convent; delirious Marguerite hears the nun admonishing her to behave politely and to accept the submissive role assigned to women:

> Une femme n'a pas besoin d'armes pour se défendre. Toujours un galant homme surgit à ses côtés pour la protéger. Vous avez eu tort d'offenser votre protecteur, M. de Roberval. (Hébert 1990, 235)

> [A woman has no need of weapons to defend herself. A gentleman will always appear at her side to protect her. You were wrong to offend your protector, M. de Roberval.]

Marguerite, on the other hand, declares that she will not bow anymore, and reiterates her wish of death upon Roberval: "[j]e lui crève les yeux et je lui perce le Coeur" (Hébert 1990, 235) [I put his eyes out and I pierce his heart]. It is in this final state that Marguerite seems to experience ultimate liberation, and it is then that she has a trance-like vision of her tormentor's murder. We learn subsequently that Roberval has died in a way similar to that prescribed by the heroine, while the circumstances surrounding his killing remain mysterious: this seems to constitute the most obvious suggestion of "supernatural" in the play. Cambron observes that the play's threatening and ominous atmosphere and its evocation of ritual murder move the story away from the moralistic tale of female religious devotion told by Marguerite de Navarre in her *Heptaméron*, and transforms the heroine into a witch-like figure who uses magic to bring about the punishment of the villain, Roberval (203).

The achievement of revenge for the wrongs done to her, and the feat of surviving the harsh conditions of life on the island, do conjure up an altered and empowered vision of the heroine. The female figure, persecuted unjustly, becomes a symbol of strength and rebellion for women, through her rejection of the oppressive patriarchal structures of her society. By the end of the play, Marguerite's description of herself "parallels the initial description of the dry, rocky, uninhabitable island" (Nyatetu-Waigwa 192). She has become "racornie comme du vieux cuir, intraitable comme la pierre" (Hébert 1990, 246) [as tough as old leather, as inflexible as rock]. This final symbolic assimilation of the female protagonist to the rugged wilderness of the island is performed through the renaming of the latter "île de la Demoiselle." The untamed wilderness and the animalised female body thus become one, in an act of inscription which questions traditional understanding of the (colonial) values of civilisation. Hébert also carries out a re-appropriation of Marguerite's story on Quebecois terms by rewriting it into a version which is very different from the original French one. She suggests an acceptance of the wilderness and of the powers of transformation it has to offer which definitely belongs to a contemporary vision, while her denunciation of women's (oppressed) social status denotes a modern approach to the story which is absent from its sixteenth-century version.

In *La cage* and *L'Île de la Demoiselle*, Anne Hébert addresses the difficulty in re- interpreting the past, and women's past in particular, by denouncing the oppressive patriarchal social structures which have governed and persecuted women's lives throughout time. Hébert's re-visiting and re-writing of the famous incident of *la Corriveau*'s story raises questions as to the authority of history writing through her use of the fairy tale form, and highlights the gender, class and cultural prejudices which repress the heroine and almost claim her life. *La cage* shows how a foreign magistrate, a stranger to the land and its customs, has power of life and death over the rural Quebecois community. Crebessa's hostility towards the rough wilderness of the New World clearly symbolises his unfitness to rule the province, and is contrasted to Ludivine's harmonious and loving relationship with Nature. Moreover, Crebessa not only embodies the disruptive foreign conqueror but also the misogynistic social bias against women frequently encountered in this era. Crebessa is therefore the ultimate persecutor in the play, the embodiment of the sufferings inflicted upon the Quebecois people, and upon women, by the foreign patriarchal authority.

Similarly in *L'Île de la Demoiselle*, Hébert presents us with the tyrannical figure of Jean-François La Roque de Roberval and denounces the colonial nature of his desire to possess the heroine's body. He also pays with his life for unfairly victimising Marguerite, who emerges victorious, if altered, from her ordeal.

Her relationship to the natural world is more testing than Ludivine's, but the potential for change it offers is also more rewarding: Marguerite reaches an "animalised" state where she is stripped of the constraints of civilisation and liberated from its gender prejudices. Hébert thus succeeds in condemning the injustices of the past and in challenging Quebec's imagined narrative by telling the stories of Marguerite and Ludivine from the perspective of the oppressed female character. As a result, both heroines are given modern voices and invested with the power to control their destinies.

NOTES

1. For the details of this *fait divers*, see Lacourcière, L. "Le triple destin de Marie-Josephte Corriveau (1733-1763)," *Cahiers des Dix*, 33, 1968.
2. For the details of this story, see Russell, D. "Quatre versions d'une légende canadienne," *Canadian Literature*, 94, 1982.
3. My translation. All further translations of the plays will be my own.
4. A version of *la Corriveau*'s story claims that she killed as many as seven husbands, and that her ghost, still imprisoned in its cage, appears to travellers at night. See Philippe-Joseph Aubert de Gaspé's novel *Les anciens Canadiens*. Quebec City, 1863.
5. See also Hajdukowski-Ahmed, M. "La sorcière dans le texte (québécois) au féminin," *The French Review*, 58: 2, 1984.
6. In this context, Luc Lacourcière points out that the original death sentence, as it was given to Joseph Corriveau, Marie-Josephte's father, did not make any mention of

the body being hung in a cage. This modality seems to have been added especially for Marie-Josephte (1968, 234).

WORKS CITED

Cambron, M. "*La cage*, suivi de *L'Île de la Demoiselle*," *Cahiers de théâtre JEU*, 60, 1991.

Green, M. *Women and Narrative Identity: Rewriting the Quebec National Text*. Montreal, 2001.

Hajdukowski-Ahmed, M. "La sorcière dans le texte (québécois) au féminin," *The French Review*, 58: 2, 1984.

Hébert, A. *Kamouraska*. Paris, 1970.

——. *Le premier jardin*. Paris, 1988.

——. *La cage*, suivi de *L'Île de la Demoiselle*. Montreal, 1990.

Knight, K. *Anne Hébert: In Search of the First Garden*. New York, 1998.

Lacourcière, L. "Le triple destin de Marie-Josephte Corriveau (1733-1763)", *Cahiers des Dix*, 33, 1968.

McKay, M. "Le pouvoir masculin contrarié: La confrontation entre la femme et l'histoire dans *La cage* et *L'Île de la Demoiselle* d'Anne Hébert," *Études francophones*, 13: 1, 1998.

Merler, G. "Cage de fer," *Canadian Literature*, 133, 1992.

Nyatetu-Waigwa, W. "The Female Liminal Place, or Survival Between the Rock and the Hard Place: A Reading of Anne Hébert's *L'Île de la Demoiselle*," in *The Art and Genius of Anne Hébert: Essays on Her Works; Night and the Day Are One*, ed J. Pallister. Madison, 2001.

O'Meara, M. "Living with the Cultural Legacy of La Corriveau: *La cage*", in *The Art and Genius of Anne Hébert: Essays on Her Works; Night and the Day Are One*, ed J. Pallister. Madison, 2001.

Rea, A. "Marie-Josephte Becomes Ludivine: The Family Reformed in Anne Hébert's *La cage*," in *Doing Gender:*

Franco-Canadian Women Writers of the 1990s, eds P. Gilbert and R. Dufault. Madison, 2001.

Russell, D. "Quatre versions d'une légende canadienne," *Canadian Literature*, 94, 1982.

Saint-Martin, L. "Écriture et combat féministe: Figures de la sorcière dans l'écriture des femmes au Québec," *Québec Studies*, 12, 1991.

The Red Dress in Hébert's
Late Novels

Deborah Hamilton

Anne Hébert wrote the short, dense dramas *Aurélien, Clara, Mademoiselle, et le Lieutenant anglais* and *Est-ce que je te dérange?* one after the other, in 1995 and 1998. In tone and narrative they differ vastly. The first, a dark fable set in rural Québec before and during World War II, traces a girl's sexual awakening. The latter, a post-modern collage, begins in contemporary Paris with the death of a homeless woman, then recoils in time. One evocative symbol appears in both: a red, unevenly-hemmed dress worn by the respective heroines Clara and Delphine. This dress might signal to the reader that the heroines are linked; and related, that Clara is Delphine's grandmother, and has handed down the dress to her. With this in mind, the novels – different as they are – stack up neatly, following each other. Both books center on seduction and abandonment. Because of Hébert's rich intertextuality, the dress image reflects seed themes of her earlier works. This essay explores this dress, and the role it plays in the seduction drama.

Clara in *Aurélien, Clara, Mademoiselle et le Lieutenant anglais* (*ACMLA*) wears a dress which is "longue par derrière, courte par-devant" (46). Her dresses were gifts to her from her schoolteacher, a mother surrogate. Fifty years later, Delphine in *Est-ce que je te dérange?* (*EQD*) wears a worn, faded pink dress left to her by her grandmother, which is "trop courte par-devant and pendante par-derrière" (66). As both dresses were given by an older woman to a young girl before her first sexual encounter, they represent learned female teachings and attitudes toward sexuality; which can be understood by looking at the dresses' color, style and fabric.

Colour

Hébert almost always uses a spare palette, favoring variations of light and dark, or black and white, with accents of red, blue, green, and gold emphasizing tensions. These black-and-white backgrounds portray harsh, dualistic values of yes-or-no worlds, such as the vast white snowfields and the black horse, sleigh and the dark outlines of winter trees in *Kamouraska*. Red blood-soaked skins on the floor of the sleigh signal drama to the reader as well as to those characters who see them, and who later testify at the murder trial. Clara in *ACMLA* is born into a mainly monotone world where a bad shadow falls on her house and her father is often in a black hole. Much of *EQD* takes place in the Parisian St-Sulpice neighborhood; besides grounding the novel in a recognizable setting, this reinforces the sober coloring, as the adjective "sulpicien," while referring to the St-Sulpice congregation or the religious art sold nearby, also translates to "dont l'idéalisation et le bariolage sont de mauvais goût."[1] We see Paris, the City of Light, largely in shades of grey.

Delphine's pink dress stands out against this plainness. Annabelle Rea explains red as the "la couleur qui symbolise la passion et la force vitale [et qui] représente une sorte de signature d'Anne Hébert pour désigner ses femmes passionnées, dionysiques" ("La femme dionysique" 103). Her women wear red accessories, such as the long scarf which floats behind Lydie as she passes on horseback in *L'Enfant chargé de songes*. Running away from home, androgynous Miguel in *Un habit de lumière* (*HL*) lugs a red suitcase containing his mother's blush. Lesser female characters often have freckles or reddish hair. The presence of these lesser characters hints at the beginnings of passion, and the red dresses worn by principal characters indicate that the passion has progressed to seduction, which will ultimately leads to death. *Héloïse*'s vampire wears red to attract victims in the Paris métro. In *Kamouraska* Aurélie is coaxed into a red velvet dress to seduce (and poison) Elisabeth's husband. Miguel in *HL* explains this red cloth's symbolism as he describes his father's anger: "il était tout rouge comme un torchon qu'on agite devant le taureau pour l'exciter" (*HL* 41). Clara and Delphine's dresses mark their entry into a cycle of sexuality and death of which they are both seducers and victims.

Of course red is the color of blood and the heart, both of which appear frequently in the texts, sometimes as figures of speech ("À coeur de jour, à coeur de nuit" [*ACMLA* 33]), often as surreal or dramatic objects. In the first pages of *Est-ce que je te dérange?* Delphine's heart is cut from her body and weighed; earlier she stayed at a hotel on rue Gît-le-Coeur where the sound of a huge heart beating in the walls kept her from sleeping. Clara's emotions are communicated by descriptions of her heart. The heroines "follow their hearts" as they act out their inner desires.

Rivers and other natural bodies of water serve almost as exterior manifestations of the body's circulatory system; as if they were external organs. Clara, Delphine and Miguel feel an organic connection to a river or a fountain. Clara "était venue à confondre le propre battement de sa vie avec la pulsation de la rivière" (65). In *ACMLA* the river serves as a central marker for the characters' displacements. The phrase "au bord de la rivière" repeats ten times in the book's 89 pages. Clara was born in a fountain of blood, while Delphine emerges from the edge of the St-Sulpice fountain, and returns there often in *EQD*. She is transfixed by the Seine, wears Petit Bateau underwear, and is compared to a fish or to a shipwreck. After her death, the fountain murmurs in Édouard's apartment. A symbol of the infinite, luminescent fountains surge at the intersection of air – the heavens – and the earth. When Delphine sits at the fountain's edge, she is at the edge of death.

Red is crucial in Hébert's thematic of what Janis Pallister names "the crisis of conflictual duality and the fusion of contrasts" ("Introduction" 43) where opposing poles of many binary oppositions, such as light/dark, night/day, male/female, silence/noise, solid/liquid, pepper the text. Lucille Roy, in her extensive work on Hébert's symbolic landscapes, presents a non-dualistic, cosmic model of it in which a continual, cyclic movement of rising and falling, joining and separating, occurs between any two poles. This movement is simultaneously creative and deadly, and it occurs in recognizable stages. Red appears at moments when oppositions are about to collapse; for example, "le feu opère la transition entre le monde extérieur et la vie intime" (Roy 185). Pink and red shades mark sunsets and dawns, as the transitional moment between night and day; while blood accompanies the transformations of birth and death, and is a universal symbol for a woman's initiatory sexual encounter: her transformational moment between girl and woman.

The color red also reminds us that Clara and Delphine are women of mixed blood; they are partially Native American or "*peaux rouges*," and their lovers are white, European men. This recalls Aurélie, in *Kamouraska*, who is half-Native American; perhaps an ancestor of Aurélien, Clara's father, who is struck by an "illumination sauvage" (9) and shuns civilization to live with the baby Clara papoose-style on his back. Aurélie wears braids while Delphine also wears braids in Paris, a style Miguel in *HL* copies playing dress-up, when he wears a pair of black tights on his head. In *Kamouraska* we see the Catholic Quebecois myth that savage, sexual, creative native women bring babies to civilized, pure, repressed white women. Aurélie wears "mince jupes," and, as Michèle Anderson points out, her "clothing clings naturally to her body, revealing her sensuality. It contrasts with the artificial stays, corsets, petticoats, and other inhibitions of the wealthy nineteenth century woman's wardrobe. [. . .] Aurélie represents the freedom of action that is forbidden" to them. (Anderson 44) Indigenous characters flash a danger to white, European audiences; firstly because the European literature has so often classified the aborigine as a savage enemy to be defeated (for example, in "cowboy and indian" stories) and, on a deeper level, as a disturbing reminder of repressed racism, extreme domination, and genocide. The duality between red and white in these novels can be read as a representation of the schisms between white and native cultures. If Delphine is wearing her grandmother Clara's red dress, it has faded to pink not only by time, but also by 50 years of socialization by white culture.

Whiteness is often introduced with severe natural phenomena such as freezing snow, disorienting fog, or blinding light. "Trop de lueurs," says Édouard, complaining of headaches and low spirits (*EQD* 34). The English Lieutenant has white skin, as does Mademoiselle, the schoolteacher who brings western culture to Clara in the whitewashed schoolhouse. The Lieutenant's internalized judges wear white wigs, while in the Québec forest, logged trees display white wounds. In *EQD* Delphine finds Parisian apartments "Badigeonnés de blanc [. . .] comme pour une laiterie de campagne" (32). The apartment of Patrick and his wife is "blanc, brilliant comme une baignoire cheminée de marbre blanc mat, le feu dans la cheminée comme un point rouge de cigarette allumé dans tout le blanc de partout ailleurs dans l'appartement blanc, la

75

moquette blanche, frissée comme un mouton, une espèce de ville blanche" (55).

Spaces where red and white co-exist mark scenes of failure, such as the checked table where Clara and the Lieutenant have a last, lonely tea, and the dress "comme une grosse fleur rouge et blanc qui s'affaise et se plie sur sa tige" (*EQD* 101) of Farida,[2] an immigrant maid fired for speaking up for herself. Similarly, the Lieutenant eats Campbell's soup for his last supper, the label of which splits into two clearly delineated bands of red and white. Negative connotations of blending red and white duplicate the thematic belief wherein love – blending male and female – leads to death; that "le couple est un enfer untenable" (Brulotte, p. 237). This agrees with Roy's model, which sees the collapse of oppositions as a continual movement of fusion and disintegration.

This conflict between the sexes can be understood through the progression of how the color is used in the two linked texts. Before each of the heroines in the later novels meets their respective lover, a red flash marks the broaching of the male/female duality. Delphine, meeting Patrick, sees "la montagne avec les érables allumés de-ci, de-là sur le vert noir des sapins" (*EQD* 48). Clara's hands are stained red from picking strawberries when she comes across the Lieutenant. The Lieutenant first sees Clara as an approaching spot of red and Delphine stands out in Paris as a pinkish blur. But these moments of sexual awakening are the result of a process in both characters and their stories, marked through the shifting use of color.

Born in a "fontaine de sang" (10) Clara spends her infancy dressed in white "lange" and "linge" in *Clara, Aurélien, Mademoiselle, et le Lieutenant anglais.* Her father wraps her in a faded, colorless sweater. She attends school because she's irresistibly attracted to the reddish glints coming from the teacher's hair, glasses, and the coloured maps on the walls. The other students laugh at her dresses "écourtichées ressemblaient à des sacs d'indienne délavés" (20) yet she is a star pupil, absorbing all of the teacher's knowledge. Mademoiselle gives Clara her belongings – including her dresses – before she dies violently, coughing and bathing Clara again in blood.

Over the years, in Clara's attic, the dresses take on a life of their own, "pendues au mur [. . .] balancées doucement, respirant dans l'ombre et paraissant vivantes. Et voici que peu à peu les robes de Mademoiselle se fanaient et devenaient minces comme du papier de soie" (34). Selling strawberries as an adolescent she meets the Lieutenant. He is attracted to her because of "sa robe d'indienne déteinte, longue par-derrière, courte par devant" (46) and the scent which escapes from beneath it. He buys all her fruit. They part and mutually obsess as a storm brews outside. Clara decides to marry him, and carefully chooses a dress to wear. She chooses a "jupe et corsage d'un rouge un peu fané, avec des sursauts de couleur au creux de plis" (68). Dressed and made up, she bicycles to him, low tree branches dampening her skirt, deepening the color and foreshadowing sex. He finds the dress too long but is seduced by her scent and they make love. She wants to stay, he grows distant. Their

77

final scene is short: "La table de la cuisine entre eux. La toile cirée à carreaux rouge et blanc. Elle a remise sa robe froissée" (82). Silent and stunned, she returns to her father's farm where the storm has covered the countryside with white foam.

Clara begins life in red, then is dressed in white, followed by faded, colorless cloth, then in faded short skirts. She is bathed in blood at Mademoiselle's death, wears a faded calico half-short, half-long skirt, then a red, long one. At the end, the world is covered in white. As a girl she wears short skirts, as an adolescent a half-short and half-long skirt, and a long dress for her entry into womanhood.

Est-ce que je te dérange? begins with Delphine's sudden death in the bed of Édouard, a Parisian who writes blurbs for a mail-order furniture catalog. Upset, he replays their conversations in his mind. We learn her story in reverse, as she reveals more about herself in her later conversations. We first see her covered in a white sheet. White-bloused men arrive to take her, then Édouard begins his recall. He first saw her in pink "au bord de la fontaine, dans la lueur des marroniers roses allignés sur la place de Saint-Sulpice" (25). She is pregnant, homeless, and confused: "[. . .][S]a robe rose, à croire que les marroniers déteigneront sur elle [. . .] elle ressemblent une grappe gonflée [. . .] courte par-devant, longue par derrière [. . .] la même robe de plus en plus défraichie. Elle s'excuse, assure qu'elle n'entre plus dans ses autres vêtements, sauf cette robe rose qui lui a offerte sa grand-mère il y a déjà longtemps" (35-50).

Delphine's clipped sentences mimic the shorthand of Édouard's advertising copy. She speaks often of her grandmother and of her heritage, consisting of money and the dress. Both are getting thinner. "[. . .] usée jusqu'à la corde [. . .] l'héritage de sa grand-mère qui s'amenuise [. . .] sa robe n'est plus qu'un chiffon sur sa peau. [. . .] 'Je suis sûr que toutes ces personnes m'ont jugée et condamnée comme une salope à cause de mon ventre et de ma robe trop courte par devant et pendante par-derrière' " (66-87). The eldest of more than fifteen children she was taken in by her grandmother who lived in a cabin by a raging river.

After her grandmother's death Delphine comes to Paris shadowing Patrick, her first lover, a married traveling salesman. She gives birth, but the midwife declares the pregnancy false, a hysteric symptom. Delphine tosses the dress. "Aux cabinets ma robe rose," she says (97), and she declares that her love for Patrick is also over. She continues to visit Édouard, in a new dress which looks like a large lampshade, and then in faded jeans and a stale t-shirt. She spends the night, and dies in his bed. Delphine's death leads him to confront his own buried past. We find out his mother's name was Rose, again evoking a shade of red. Thus, as the narrative travels backwards in time searching for Dolphin's secrets, it makes a parallel journey to unlock Édouard's. Perhaps Hébert is suggesting that all of us share the same core.

Delphine begins the book in white, then appears in faded clothes, and lives in the pink dress for months of her pregnancy. At her birth scene we imagine blood, and then she wears the new dress of an unspecified bright shade ("vive" as opposed to stale). Later she's in faded jeans and t-shirt again before dying under white sheets. She progresses from white to faded to pink to blood to bright, then back to faded, and back to white. Both women, then, move on a continuum from white to red, and then fade again into white. Red marks their moment of sexual initiation and desire, as well as birth and death.

Clothing as Symbolic Link

There are other clues that support a grandmother-granddaughter link between Clara and Delphine. Delphine's memories of her grandmother's cabin, mentioned above, sound exactly like Clara's childhood home. Delphine talks obsessively about her grandmother, her only source of love, emphasizing their closeness. "Là d'où je viens, c'était ma grand-mère, rien que ma grand-mère," she says (102). "Elle prononce 'ma grand-mère' lentement, avec précaution, comme s'il s'agissait d'un mot précieux et fragile et sa figure devient claire. Elle [. . .] est tout à fait joyeuse" (39).

Secondly, both women have similar wild child behavior. Like the character in Truffaut's film, Clara cannot speak or read until age ten nor can Delphine maintain a dialogue. Both move tirelessly. Julia Douthwaite describes, in her study of feral children in the eighteenth and nineteenth centuries, how Europeans were shocked by the way wild children devoured hunks of raw meat.[3] *EQD* shows us "Delphine chez la grand-mère qui lui montre comment dépiauter une cuisse de poulet avec ses dents" (125). Clara thinks in metaphors wherein small animals devour each other; she imitates their calls perfectly before she can talk. As rural, poor Quebecoise, both women represent the savage Other to civilized Europeans. But the dress is the clue which suggests that Clara is the grandmother who raised Delphine.

Hébert dresses her characters in garments which mirror their roles, and which often serve to represent that character, her essence, or life force. Mademoiselle pulls Clara's wool cap over her ears when she wants Clara to obey her, sheeplike. Rose-Alba in *HL* wears a red hunting jacket to sleuth out her missing son. Aggressive and selfish, she wants a fur coat. Clothing can be a concealing veil, or it can sensually reveal and highlight bodies and their movements. Male characters are attracted to the short skirts of Native American women. In "Un Grand Mariage," an early story from *Le Torrent*, the protagonist compares his white wife, lost in her skirts and shawls, and the fussiness and encumbrance of her skirts and petticoats, which require bleaching, pleating, starching, washing, etc. to the natural ease and erotic appeal of his Native American lover. The poem "La chambre fermée" gives another skirt image.

> Et toute la rose du feu
> En ses jupes pourpres gonflées
> Autour de son coeur possédé et gardé
> Sous les flammes [. . .] (12-15)

Puffed skirts suggest dance, and couples stepping in predetermined roles, while other phrases hint of passion, possession, and female genitalia. In its entirety, the poem describes violent sacrifice.

As the doctor signing Delphine's death certificate cross-examines Édouard, the copywriter thinks, "deux ou trois choses que je sais d'elle" (18). This is the title of a 1967 Godard film, about which the director made the famous quote, "quand on soulève les jupes de la ville, on en voit le sexe." In the film a woman becomes a prostitute not out of poverty, but because she feels driven to buy dresses and other advertised consumer goods. "Elle" in the title refers to Paris, which, according to Godard, changed in the 1960s. Godard felt that everyone in the new Paris was forced to prostitute themselves in some way. Due to Delphine's odd behavior, her long hours walking the streets, and her sudden death at 23, the doctor suspects her of streetwalking. Earlier, Édouard had sent her to a cheap hotel used by prostitutes. She thinks that others see her as a "salope" (66). Clara, until *ACMLA*'s last pages, is a virgin, while Delphine, only a few years older and barely more experienced, is seen as a whore. Earning a living in a commercial age is a central theme in *EQD*, where jobs are meaningless and unsatisfying. Édouard "tape des inepties pour le compte d'un catalogue de vente par correspondance. [. . .] Est-ce donc ainsi que les hommes vivent?" (49).

A hooker's short skirt exaggerates woman's traditional dress. Only very recently have trousers been acceptable for western women; and many civil and religious customs still frown on them. Pauline in *Bur-

den of Dreams, tired of her husband, "committed the first transgression [. . .] Giving up skirts and petti-coats" to wear trousers (33-34). Her husband soon leaves her and others regard her suspiciously.

Fabric choice offers more clues. Clara's first dress-es are of faded "indienne" (calico), underscoring her mixed race and also her poverty, because they look like flour sacks. Mademoiselle's dresses are "en soie." "L'en soi" is the existential term for the unconscious, and in psychoanalysis "le soi" refers to interiorized, unconscious drives. These women act from strong inner pulsions. Selling strawberries, Clara feels a force stronger than the wind pushing her. Delphine runs from her dead grandmother's house, pushed, she explains, by "une sorte d'obligation plus fort que tout. Un entêtement effrayante" (*EQD* 67).

The threadbare quality of Delphine's pink dress shows her precarious condition; she's close to death, as Miguel is in *HL* when he says "le temps invivable dans lequel je suis s'amincit comme une étoffe usée" (120). Delphine compares the distorting Paris fog to the thick, webby fluffiness of white cotton batting. "On s'enfarge dans du coton," she says (*EQD* 47). When she flew from Canada, the jet passed through clouds. "De l'ouate partout . . . J'étouffe," she com-plained. Miguel is "à moitié suffoqué dans l'aube cotonneuse" (*HL* 111).

There are other fabrics, such as "le velours rouge et la mousseline blanche" (HL 112) which decorate Jean's platform bed. "Mousseline" is white, filmy, and light, the stuff of wedding dresses, and it carries over-tones of "mousse," foam or moss, natural elements from the outdoors. It protects baby Clara from mosquitos. "Mousse" also means soft.[4] Jean-Ephrem's impotency in *HL* causes Rose-Alba's "robe de mousseline" to be "gonflée de colère plus éclatante que les murs cramoisis" (116). A lover of luxurious fabrics, when Rose-Alba is desperate she promises God that she'll become "vierge à jamais sous la bure et le voile." (122) "Bure" is the rough, homespun cloth of monks' tunics.

Lines also connect binary pairs. There is a line between life and death ("la fine jointure de la vie et de la mort" [*EQD* 48]) and the line of the horizon ("[le] ciel écarlate qui est au bout de l'enfer comme une bordure de flammes claires" [119]). Delphine watches a fisherman by the Seine. "La ligne [. . .] se tend. Un petit poisson frétille au bout de la ligne. Le pêcheur tremble de joie de la tête aux pieds" (48). The fishing line connects the fisherman and his prey, a fish. Both tremble: one in joy, one in death. This mimics the connection between Patrick, fishing tackle salesman, with his suitcase of "hameçons et mouches," and Delphine, "comme une limande" (91). When Delphine is at her lowest point, dying, Patrick is at his highest, happily on vacation with his wife. Lines and ties also symbolize binding social obligations. Patrick swears to Delphine that he loves her, but he is tied to his wife. A "ligne d'ancêtres" (*ACMLA* 48) press themselves in Clara's veins and prevent her from speaking her unique, individual voice.

Janis Pallister traces Hébert's knot and cord imagery to fifteenth and sixteenth century black arts, which often used needles and knots. The nun Julie casts spells in *Les Enfants du sabbat*, which result in deaths and a stillborn baby ("Cord and Knot Imagery" 226). This gives a new perspective to Delphine's mysterious pregnancy in *EQD*, as Patrick's ogress wife seems to be totally in control. "Je suis dévorante et tout ce que je convoite m'appartient déjà," (86), she says, and vows to adopt Delphine's baby. Did she cast a spell on Delphine so that the child would die, or did she steal it after its birth, as Delphine suspects? Was Patrick sent to Québec with his suitcase of fishing lures in search of a surrogate mother for his child, per his wife's design? Was Delphine sacrificed for their needs? *ACMLA* also hints at black magic. Mademoiselle singles Clara out and casts a spell on her. Pine needles crunch under Clara's feet on the path to the Lieutenant's cabin. Clara "pique et repique son aiguille dans la tissu rêche d'une vieille jupe" (67). Was she casting a spell? If this old skirt is the one she wore to her encounter with the Lieutenant, it becomes a magical instrument, a charm, a lure, and if this is the same skirt which Delphine wears fifty years later, it's no wonder that she attracts Patrick, Édouard, and Stéphane.

Intertwined with the images of clothing, fruit metaphors evolve from one novel to another. In *ACMLA*, we see Clara and "son innnocence comme un fruit vert à cueillir" (73). Delphine is a full, swollen grape, and then, "mûre comme un fruit trop mûr [. . .] prêt à tomber par terre" (87), while the angelic Mademoiselle resembles a dead leaf as she dies. Each woman's clothes are stored in an appropriate way for these fruits. Clara's hang on clotheslines, similar to swaying trees, and Mademoiselle's hang from a nail. *Clouer* carries the sense of being paralyzed by fear, and of crucifixion. Clothing of those who are dying is scattered on the ground, and falling into the earth.

Clara's garments on the clothesline are pulled and suspended by cords and lines, just as she is pulled through life, puppet-like. Pulsions or drives, pulleys and ropes, pulses of the heart and of the river, these images loop and overlap in the texts where characters, whether pulled, nailed, or falling earthward, are not free.

The distinguishing detail in Clara and Delphine's red dress is its length: short-in-front, long-in-back. Girls wear short dresses while women, especially in past years, wear long skirts. Clara and Delphine's half-long, half-short dresses suggest their adolescent status, as well as being half-Native American, half-white; and half-modern, half old-fashioned. The short front is sexy and revealing while the long back hides.

Of course, the short front could be lifted intentionally, while stepping up or down, while curtseying, or while being seductive. Héloïse "relève ses jupes et jupons à pleines mains" (*Heloïse* 100) when she seduces Bernard, yet the cold wife in "Un grand mariage" makes a similar gesture of gathering her skirts about her so that her husband can pass, thus dismissing him.[5] It is not clear who seduces who. The Lieutenant is obsessed with Clara's scent, hidden beneath her dress, and the purchase of her strawberries would seem suggestive; however, he has tried to put her out of his mind. She recognizes and acts by going to him, wearing a dress, symbolically described previously as being alive, in order to seduce him. In *EQD* we first see Delphine as innocent and needy, running by the side of the road where Patrick comes to her aid. Then a surprising line shifts the perspective, suggesting Patrick's guilt. Une "lueur de verrière pénètre dans la petite auto cahotante quand il lui offre des bonbons" (72). We all know that you shouldn't take candy from strangers, and the lure of a sunbeam spotlights this fact and adds to the drama. Yet, a hitchhiker in an alluring red dress is also suspicious; Delphine starts to look like an active party in the seduction.

Michel Foucault says that seduction – coercing another into sex – as well as the accompanying shame and silence, are conditioned responses to modern taboos. Earlier, he posits, freely consensual sex was neither shamed nor hidden. Seduction games are the result of modern loneliness and alienation. Because all characters in Hébert's late novels are extremely lonely and alienated, it's no surprise that they are vulnerable to seduction. As Delphine says, "tout le monde est seul" (*EQD* 107).

Although he swears that "cette fille ne m'est rien" (10), the real love interest in *EQD* is between Delphine and Édouard. She comes to his bed repeatedly, and he describes them as an old couple. Patrick is the man she talks about, but it's Édouard she shadows, and who is "dérangé" by her presence. She wears the pink dress during most of their time together, and he crosses the line that separates them to meet her. "J'établis une nette frontière, en plein milieu du lit, une sort de *no man's land* où il vaut mieux ne pas se risquer" (109) he says, then he crosses it to touch her breasts.

The novels contain a great deal of textile terminology. Clara sews, her stitches standing in for words, as she prepares to meet her lover. Rose-Alba works away at a deafening pace at her sewing machine. The doctor checks Delphine's arms for needle marks. Woven cloth is a network of intersecting lines, or threads. Édouard plans to "[R]etrouver le fil d'un texte commencé la veille. Aligner des mots" (21). Delphine is "folle à lier" (113). In French a hem is an "ourlet" or "bord," an edge or a border. Borders, imaginary lines or frontiers, abound in the novels; as was earlier noted, "au bord de" repeats frequently in *ACMLA*. Hems are margins, and these characters are marginalized, exploitable people. That so many of Hébert's protagonists are 15-year-olds shows the importance, and delicacy of crossing the line from child to adult. The Lieutenant muses about "Petites filles qui dépassent la frontière et rejoignent la coherte de grandes personnes" (*ACMLA* 59). Crossing this line, and simultaneously the one between male and female, is likened to "Un bruit de soie qui crisse et se déchire [. . .]" (81).

A two-sided, uneven skirt also comments on modern women's dual options – Madonna or whore – in a society controlled by patriarchal institutions. Women are encouraged to be attractive and flirtatious, but often persecuted or shamed when they do so. Rose-Alba is punished for wearing a short skirt which shows her legs, because her husband feels that her body is his property. He rips the dress, and promises to buy her a new one, and, obediently, she swears it will be long.

Similarly, Patrick is ashamed of Delphine's dress when they are in public together, so he buys her an ankle-length coat to hide her swollen shape, too suggestive of sexuality and of his guilt. She takes it off when he leaves, but "[. . .] quand il me sort [. . .] je le garde tout le temps. J'étouffe de chaleur. Mais je fais comme il veux" (*EQD* 57).

Yet when clothing is a gift between women, it can carry a different, more altruistic message. Mademoiselle gives Clara her heritage: "C'est pour toi. Tout est pour toi" (25). In addition to the material objects, Mademoiselle teaches her communication, music, literature, other practical skills; and the values of generosity and solidarity. Clara in turn gives love, peace, nurturing, and overwhelming love to Delphine. Traveling between three women, the dress is a talisman of love and support. None of the three women receive similar nurturing from men.

Hébert Coming Full Circle

The focus of this paper has been Hébert's two penultimate novels, but also shows how Hébert has consistently used similar, yet evolving imagery to illustrate her themes. Looking back at two of her earliest works, we can see how Hébert closes the symbolic narrative she began as early at the 1930s with her later novellas, as well as returning to a shorter form of storytelling. "La robe corail," was written in 1939. Again, it describes a young girl's seduction and awakening. Silent and naive Emilie works at a knitting workshop with other flirtatious, pretty girls who wear short skirts. A passing woodsman, Gabriel, leaves her a colored image which makes her laugh. Like Clara, she is seduced by colors, and feels called to join a mysterious rite. She begins to knit a coral dress for a client, and her life changes, becoming dreamy and magical. "La laine vive glissait sur les aiguilles d'os, le rêve, plus vif encore, glisse en gouttes insaisissables dans le coeur" (70). The dress grows and Gabriel serenades her, singing of eternal love. The wool also talks to her: "[. . .] c'est drôle ce qu'elle raconte" (70).

When the dress is finished, she tries it on and it fits like a jewel, except that it's too short. Gabriel climbs to her window and carries her off. In the forest, they lie on his red-and-black checkered jacket. Amorous at night, in the morning he turns cold. Emilie goes to work, and hears, from the others, that he's returning to his (previously unmentioned) fiancée.

Emilie's metamorphosis from grey to coloured results from her knitting. She glows, jewel-like, in her coral dress. Delphine also resembles a lampshade (which glows) at one point. A lampshade can be read literally as "abat-jour," kill the day. Delphine dies soon after throwing away her red dress in favor of the lampshade model. Like Miguel, she ends her life in a suit of light. Emilie is carried off by Gabriel to a death of sorts enacted on a checkerboard. As Miguel explained, the red cloth flashed in front of a bull is a fatal lure.

The haunting novella *Le Torrent* was written in 1945. The young couple enact a seduction drama, and at the end, we're unable to fix guilt or blame on any of them: the oppressed, abusive mother? The damaged son? Devilish Amica? All are victims and all are guilty. Perspective shifts fluidly and often, collapsing oppositions as in this description of a woman's dress, is filled with swirling, watery metaphors.

> Ses jupes et châles la drapent et ne semblent retenus que par les agrafes mouvantes de ses mains, plus ou moins serrées, selon les caprices de sa démarche vive ou nonchalante. Un réseau de plis glissent de ses mains et renaissant plus loin en ondes pressées. Jeux des plis et des mains. Noeud de plis sur la poitrine en une seule main. Scintillement de soie trop tendue sur les épaules. Equilibre rompu, recrée ailleurs. Glissement de soie, épaule nue, dévoilement des bras. Doigts si bruns sur la jupe route. La jupe est relevée à poignées, prestement, pour monter l'escalier. Les chevilles sont fines, les jambes parfaites. Un genou saillit. Tout est disparu. La jupe balaie le plancher, les mains sont libres et le corsage ne tient plus. (*Le Torrent* 31)

Here is the dress which we've seen refracted throughout *Aurélien, Clara, Mademoiselle, et le Lieutenant anglais* and *Est-ce que je te dérange?* Red, silky, seductive, it alternatively reveals, entices and veils, driving the erotic narrative. Fabric falls in natural patterns: waves, a knot, a cascade, until, finally, the dress itself bleeds and blurs into *le torrent*, "ces eaux mystérieux et néfastes" (Roy 15) where so many of Hébert's characters die.

1. *Le Nouveau Petit Robert*. Paris: Dictionnaires Le Robert, 1991. 2428.
2. Farida, seemingly of North African origin, is the contemporary counterpart to Florida in *Kamouraska*.
3. See <http://www.FeralChildren.com/en/diet.php>
3. Interestingly, in the sixteenth century, "mousse" meant young girl. Later it evolved to signify a boy less than sixteen years old serving as an apprentice on a commercial sailing vessel. This definition is touching when fifteen-year-old Miguel, teased by his father for his girlish softness, is considered. (*Le Nouveau Petit Robert* 1627)
4. Reading about Delphine's long, observant walks in Paris, one can't help but think of Baudelaire. In his poem "A Une Passante" Baudelaire describes a woman raising her hem. "Une femme passa, d'une main fasteuse / Soulevant, balançant le feston et l'ourlet". (3-4) Another obvious Baudelaire reference is his poem "La Fontaine de Sang."

WORKS CITED

Anderson, Michèle. "Toward a New Definition of Eroticism." *The Art and Genius of Anne Hébert*. Ed. Janis L. Pallister. Madison: Fairleigh Dickinson University Press, 2001. 40-53.

Baudelaire, Charles. *Les oeuvres complètes*. Paris: Robert Laffont, 1980.

Bishop, Neil. "Amérindiens et Québécois francophones dans le film *La canne à pêche*." *The Art and Genius of Anne Hébert*. Ed. Janis L. Pallister. Madison: Fairleigh Dickinson University Press, 2001. 210-219.

Brulotte, Gaétan. "La représentation du corps chez Anne Hébert." *The Art and Genius of Anne Hébert*. Ed. Janis L. Pallister. Madison: Fairleigh Dickinson University Press, 2001. 232-250.

Douthwaithe, Julia. *The Wild Girl, Natural Man, and the Dangerous Experiments in the Age of Enlightenment.* Chicago: University of Chicago Press, 2002.

<http://www.FeralChildren.com/en/diet.php>

Foucault, Michel. *The History of Sexuality. Volume I: An Introduction.* New York: Vintage Books, 1990.

Godard, Jean-Luc. Interview. *L'avant-Scène Cinéma.* Paris: May, 1967.

Gontard, Marc. "Noir, blanc et rouge: le chromo-récit d'Anne Hébert dans *Kamouraska.*" *Anne Hébert, parcours d'une oeuvre.* Actes du colleque de la Sorbonne. Montréal: L'Hexagone. 1997.

Guillemette, Lucie. "De la fin des dogmes à la volonté de puissance du sujet féminin: une lecture nietzchéene d'*Aurélien, Clara, Mademoiselle et le lieutenant anglais.*" *Les Cahiers d'Anne Hébert* 3 (2001): 122-139.

Hébert, Anne. *Aurélien, Clara, Mademoiselle, et le lieutenant anglais.* Paris: Seuil, 1995.

Hébert, Anne. *Burden of Dreams.* Trans. Sheila Fischman. Concord: House of Anansi Pess Ltd., 1994.

——. *Est-ce que je te dérange?* Paris: Seuil, 1998.

——. *Héloïse.* Paris: Seuil, 1980.

——. *Kamouraska.* Paris: Seuil, 1970.

——. *L'Enfant chargé de songes.* Paris: Seuil, 1992.

——. *Le Torrent.* Paris: Seuil, 1963.

——. *Les Enfants du sabbat.* Paris: Seuil, 1975.

——. *Oeuvre Poétique.* Montréal: Boréal, 1992.

——. *Un habit de lumière.* Paris: Seuil, 1999.

Munley, Ellen W. "*Un habit de lumière* in the Light of Three Cultural Perspectives." *The Art and Genius of Anne Hébert.* Ed. Janis L. Pallister. Madison: Fairleigh Dickinson University Press, 2001. 121-140.

Pallister, Janis L. "Cord and Knot Imagery in *Les Enfants du sabbat.*" *The Art and Genius of Anne Hébert.* Ed. Janis L. Pallister. Madison: Fairleigh Dickinson University Press, 2001. 223-229.

——. "Introduction." *The Art and Genius of Anne Hébert*. Ed. Janis L. Pallister. Madison: Fairleigh Dickinson University Press, 2001. 121-140.

Rea, Annabelle M. "La femme dionysique chez Anne Hébert." *Les Cahiers d'Anne Hébert* 2 (2000) : 95-110.

Roy, Lucille. *Anne Hébert. Entre la Lumière et l'Ombre*. Montréal: XYZ, 2000.

Von Zwoll, Lisa R. "Mort, meurtre et maternité: "Le torrent" et *Un habit de lumière*." *Les Cahiers d'Anne Hébert* 4 (2003) : 127-145.

Chacun son diable:
Anne Hébert's Lucifer

ANNABELLE M. REA

Diabolical figures, in many and varied guises, have appeared in Anne Hébert's writing since the start of her career. The little faunlike dancer, Ysa, of "L'Ange de Dominique" (written between 1938 and 1944), tempts the eponymous adolescent to realize her dream of expressing her paralyzed body in dance. In so doing, he suggests the complicity of art with the diabolical. François Perrault of "Le Torrent" condemns the dark-skinned Amica as sexual temptress: "Amica est le diable. Je convie le diable chez moi" (34). Bestial representations of human passions, such as the black horses, Perceval of "Le Torrent" or George Nelson's "prince des ténèbres" (169) of *Kamouraska*, also occur.[1] The Parisian vampire, "le vieux démon" (54) Xavier Bottereau of *Héloïse*, might be cited as well.

The work where Hébert most openly and at length explored stereotypes of the Devil is the mid-career *Les Enfants du sabbat* (1975). Adélard – the substitution of the d for the b is surely a wink at his diabolical role – is described as "rusé, insidieux" (14), and "majestueux" (41). He directs the celebration of a Black Mass, with his nude body "barbouillé de noir" (65) and his face "plein de suie" (44). He wears a "couronne de feuilles vertes" and "deux cornes de vache" (39). He incites those present to a variety of forbidden activities: dance, drunkenness, nudity, and sex, including adultery and incest. Adélard calls himself the Devil – "il prétend qu'il est le diable" (64) – and others use that term, as well as "le dieu froid" (116), "le Malin" (101, 147, 149), "l'Autre" (150), and "Satan" (110, 119, 148).

Hébert's frequent references to the Devil are, of course, not surprising. Her education in Catholic schools would have provided regular admonitions to avoid temptation from the Evil One. In twentieth-century Catholicism, the Devil was not merely a figurative representation of evil; three popes in particular – Pius XII, Paul VI, and John Paul II – maintained his concrete existence.[2] The latter, even, reportedly, admitted to having performed an exorcism in the Vatican in 1982, less than a quarter-century ago.[3] At least until the liberation that followed the Révolution Tranquille in the 1960s, the Catholicism of Quebec, the Catholicism of Hébert's youth, remained rigidly conservative. The celebrated ecclesiastic, the prolific Lionel Groulx, wrote, for example, of "l'empire de Satan" (Serrin 368) and held steadfastly, throughout his career in the twentieth century, to late nineteenth-century principles. For Quebec's clergy, woman was the temptress; sexual activity not devoted to procreation within marriage was the work of the Devil. The role played by the Evil One in Quebec's folk tales – such as "L'Étranger," where the Devil comes to dance with Rose Latulipe, or "La Chasse-galerie," and its pact with the Devil – sums up the figure's centrality within the culture. As Aurélien Boivin, the collector and editor of many of those tales, has commented: "Satan, ange déchu, a profondément marqué l'imaginaire québécois" (*Le Conte* 13).[4]

However, the Hébertian devil I wish to discuss does not operate in a Québécois context. Instead, in her final novel, *Un habit de lumière* (1999), Hébert matched him – this devil of Hébert's, like most other representations, is male – with a Spanish family living in France. Spain's Catholicism had been the centerpiece of the Inquisition, which had continued there into the nineteenth century, much later than in other parts of the world (Stanford 182). It remained tied to the past, tied to the State, even longer than Quebec's Church, until the death of Francisco Franco in 1975.[5] Moreover, Hébert's Almevida family hails from Andalucia, a region with particular notions of the separate domains of male and female, with strict concepts of masculine "honor," and an even more conservative Church.[6] The father of the family, with his misunderstood and redundant Trinitarian self-proclamation: "Je suis le Père, le Mari, le *Pater Familias*" (36), represents this tie to conservative Catholicism, to "la vie ancienne intacte et pure" (95). It is no surprise, then, that Hébert calls him Pedro – the Rock – and that his wife and son, in their liberation from traditional values, constantly collide with the rigid obstacle he embodies.[7]

Within this context of family discord, Hébert introduced, almost half-way through the novel, a diabolical figure. This one does not perform a Black Mass, nor does he wear horns, like Adélard of *Les Enfants du sabbat*. In fact, at first, one may not realize what the "danseur étoile" (83) of a Montmartre night club represents. For me, the enlightenment came (the pun is very much intended) when I realized why Hébert had insisted three times in the space of a few pages on a "lampe minuscule" (126, 129, 132) because I saw the relationship between that little lamp and the etymology of Lucifer, the light bearer, a point to which I will return. I want, therefore, to look in some detail at this dancer who calls himself "Jean-Ephrem de la Tour," in order to better understand the role played by Hébert's diabolical figures in general and, in particular, the significance of this small gem of a novel within her overall production.

The many studies of the devil by art historians, anthropologists, theologians, and literary scholars agree on a number of characteristics illustrated by portraits of the Evil One over the centuries. A brief summary of these traits will help us understand what Hébert has done in *Un habit de lumière*, as anyone familiar with the text will realize in going through the list.

First, the physical characteristics:

the devil is almost always male

he is magnificent in his beauty: "le plus beau des anges," according to Roland Villeneuve, the major French scholar of demonology (*Dictionnaire* 559)

he is naked, or shown wearing only a loincloth or a sort of skirt (the fall from heaven, according to some, having destroyed his angelic robes)[8]

he is most often black – among his sobriquets are "the Great Negro"/"le Grand Nègre"[9] he is androgynous or bisexual[10]

he is a shape-shifter, who can take on a variety of names and disguises, including animal forms, such as those of the horse or the wolf [11]

Next, his activities, generally nocturnal, are described as disorderly, outside the bounds of civilized society. They concern, primarily, the human body, which psychotherapist Edward Tejirian has termed "the vehicle for his temptations" (169):

dance, first of all, which has long been denounced as "l'invention de Satan" (Villeneuve, *Beauté* 200)[12]

all manner of sexual activity (the Devil is known for his sexual appetites and his potency[13]), including adultery, sodomy, incest, bestiality. And, finally, the Devil has been described, morally, as:

the Great Seducer: "celui qui séduit toute la terre" (Villeneuve, *Dictionnaire* 293, 942)[14]; "the tempt[er] of the innocent" (Russell 74)

the Great Liar: "le père du mensonge"[15]

a roving trickster, immoral and unrepentant[16]

The match between Hébert's "Jean-Ephrem de la Tour" and these characteristics, although perhaps not obvious at first reading, seems remarkably exact. The dancer is described as "le plus beau de tous" (69). He performs "à moitié nu" (66). His black skin makes of him "l'Ange noir" (110) or "un roi nègre dans son château" (89).[17] Bisexual, he reports that "il n'a jamais désappointé ni une dame ni un monsieur" (108). His theatrical career allows him the shape-shifting and disguise that have long characterized portraits of the Devil. We learn that the name "Jean-Ephrem de la Tour" is but the most recent of many: "Bien mal venu celui qui tenterait de remonter la filière des noms et prénoms, perdus en cours de route, jusqu'à la DDASS originelle" (83).[18] Hébert includes animality in the list of disguises, as she compares him to a "cheval noir" (67, 103), speaks of his "étrange pupille oblique comme celle des loups" (132), shows him "méditant sa prochaine férocité" (108), admitting "j'ai fait l'Ange au théâtre et la bête au lit" (117), or has him call himself "la Belle Bête" (67, 108).[19] And, quite clearly, his nocturnal activities, both as a dancer and as a "superstud," fit within the long-established criteria. Not only has "l'Ange des Ténèbres" (66) seduced the innocent adolescent Miguel, but he also commits, or at least intends to, what has been termed an incest "of the second type" (Storms 105, n. 7): that is, when two blood relatives have a common sexual partner, by agreeing to go to bed with Miguel's mother as well.

Morally too, Hébert's dancer possesses the established traits. He is, first of all, fully aware of his seductive powers. As he invites the fifteen-year-old Miguel to his night club, Jean-Ephrem remarks: "La séduction fait son chemin" (63). He admits to fabrication: "Avouer . . . Puis enchaîner dans la pure fantaisie" (135). He speaks of his need to "vivre à grandes guides, et sans scrupule" (132). Having done his damage in Paris, he is off "toward the sun and the sea"

(135), carrying under his arm his only remaining possession, the previously mentioned "petite lampe minuscule"; the rest of his belongings have been reclaimed by his creditors.

As I have noted earlier, the insistence on the lamp reminds us that one of the names of the fallen angel was Lucifer, the light-bearer. This detail seems central to Hébert's message and it points, I think, to one specific source for Hébert's diabolical creation. I will look only briefly at that source, in seventeenth-century British literature – briefly, because, lacking knowledge of that period, I have no business going there. The detour seems necessary, however, because I hope that by my drawing attention to it, one day a comparatist will look seriously at the parallels between John Milton's *Paradise Lost* and Hébert's many references, throughout her works, to the events recounted in the poem. I should say, parenthetically, that I have verified that Hébert indeed had a copy of Milton's work in her library, now housed in the Centre Anne-Hébert at the Université de Sherbrooke.[20]

Le Paradis Perdu, the name of the Montmartre club where Jean-Ephrem performs, tips us off perhaps most obviously to the English poet's contribution. Milton stresses "splendour and magnificence" (Werblowsky 23) in his prelapsarian portrait of the angel Lucifer. The skimpy theatrical costume worn by Hébert's dancer includes "[a]iles d'argent accrochées aux épaules" (61). Hébert notes that "[Il] règne sur un peuple de danseurs et d'acrobates" (61). A gesture toward his co-workers reveals his regal power over them: "un seul geste d'un de ses grands bras levé" (74) suffices. But however splendid the Paradis Perdu appears, this "magical universe" (75), with its "aigrettes . . . , plumes . . . , strass . . . , paillettes" (68), pales in comparison with Jean-Ephrem's living quarters.

He seems to live in the sky – the heavens, of course – in his eighth-floor loft, the probable inspiration for his choice of the "de la Tour" name, full of "bizarre objects of gold and silver" (84), an apartment that "dépasse en magnificence le Paradis Perdu lui-même" (84). The dancer in his glory is, like Lucifer, the rival of God; he is hired, amusingly, "en vedette américaine" (61), that is, secondary to the main act (but that "main act" will not appear in the novel, which seems to be Hébert's very subtle way of confirming God's absence).[21] In his pride, Milton's Lucifer boasts that he is "self-begot" (Russell 101). Similarly, Jean-Ephrem says that he has never had a mother.[22] One could continue the list of parallels; I hope someone will.

Jean-Ephrem can be seen, then, as a composite of the figurations of the Devil through the ages, with particular emphasis on Milton's Lucifer. Hébert's temptation scene takes place, however, not between Satan and Eve in a paradisaical garden, but in a Paris street, where the dancer meets the adolescent Miguel. Miguel – Michael – is, of course, the name of the Archangel chosen to combat Lucifer, who has rebelled against God.[23]

Those who have readied Miguel for this encounter are, first, Pedro, his rigid, rule-bound father ("Il faut ce qu'il faut" [20]), the *Pater Familias* obsessed with virile honor, his own and his son's. Pedro imposes his standards on his son, sometimes brutally, via karate lessons and a stringent dress code. In fact, Pedro may himself be seen as a sort of demon, through his physical and psychological battering of both his son and his wife. The construction worker – a carpenter perhaps? — often away for long periods working on various building projects, sees the closeness between mother and son, a closeness characteristic of Mediterranean cultures in general, and regrets his outsider status.

The second, and primary, influence on Miguel's life is his mother Rose-Alba, whom he considers his twin, his double, his "complice."[24] Her name evokes maternal devotion, in its allusions to the "Litany of the Blessed Virgin Mary" – such as "mystical rose" and "morning star," the latter for *alba*, or white, in Latin.[25] Instead, however, Rose-Alba's gaze remains firmly fixed on herself and the realization of her material desires, as her repetition of the first person eighteen times in the first fourteen lines (the first page) of the novel announces.

Despite Miguel's closeness to his mother, a closeness with incestuous overtones,[26] he obtains no real validation from Rose-Alba. She reacts to his struggle to affirm his sexual identity, his predilection for female activities and clothing, less brutally than does her husband, but still with such insensitive comments as "Ça va pas la tête!" (16), shouted at him out into the street. She too has dreams of virile combat for her son, expressed through the heroic Spanish archetype of the bullfighter, brave before the bestial adversary. Miguel is left with only the wistful hope "that one day [his] mother will accept [him] as [he is]" (27).

It is easy to see Hébert's irony at work in this variant of the Holy Family (with the carpenter as absent father, the mother whose name evokes the Virgin Mary, and the son).[27] Certainly, this remains true in the choice of the name Miguel, for, in his oedipal desires of patricide, the son is anything but "angelic." Is is, as I have said, rather the Archangel sent to do battle with Lucifer that inspires the name. Although Michael is known in the Catholic tradition as (and here I quote John Coulson, who gives details from post-mass prayers) "captain of the Heavenly Host" and "safeguard against the wickedness and snare of the devil" (332), it has been pointed out that his combat against Lucifer was not, in fact, very successful;[28] God had to call in His Son to finish the task. In Hébert's novel, the young and vulnerable Miguel, an adolescent in search of his identity, will not survive his encounter with Lucifer.

In his relationship with Jean-Ephrem, Miguel finds comfort, usefulness, and, above all, acceptance. Comfortable in the nightclub environment ("la fête pour laquelle je suis fait" [65]), even though it is described as a sort of hell, with "des creatures de rêve . . . jetées toutes vives dans la fournaise" (91); useful as a wage earner selling flowers and as a valet to Jean-Ephrem, Miguel gains a certain maturity and self-confidence. But what matters most is Jean-Ephrem's acceptance of Miguel's sexual identity: "j'ai toujours voulu être une fille" (106), as Miguel tells him. Unlike the black and white uniform of virility imposed by Pedro or the heroic torero's costume of the book's title imagined by Rose-Alba for her son, the dress and the lingerie provided by Jean-Ephrem adorn Miguel with what he considers his truth, his "véritable image" (107).[29]

And yet the encounter with Jean-Ephrem ends tragically. Rose-Alba has invaded her son's territory, demonically, one might say. Although she knows that Miguel idolizes Jean-Ephrem – "mon fils adore cet homme qui le tourmente" (110) — she determines to go to bed with the glamorous dancer herself. Betrayed by those he loves and trusts, both his mother and Jean-Ephrem, his youthful desire for justice thwarted, Miguel throws himself into the Seine. He loved too much; he was not loved enough. Like Irène, the colorless wife of the Pastor, Nicolas Jones, of *Les Fous de Bassan*, Miguel kills himself quietly, without trying to explain his act.[30] But he, at least, dreams of future acceptance by "quelqu'un de sacré que je ne connais pas encore" (137).

What, then, can we conclude about this last incarnation of the Devil in the writing of Anne Hébert? First, I think, we can say that the rootless, classless Jean-Ephrem, the shape-shifter, can represent all things to all people. For Rose-Alba Almevida, he is all magnificence and splendor – ironically akin to Milton's Lucifer. For her, he is what Edward Tejirian has called "the lord of matter" (69). But, like Rose-Alba's own inauthenticity (the dark, chunky Spaniard aspires to be blond and slender like the bulimic Lady Di, for instance), Jean-Ephrem's glory is a sham. For Rose-Alba's son, Jean-Ephrem is finally the only one who will accept him for what he is. The dancer represents everything for the adolescent: "Enfer et paradis pour un enfant qui s'ennuie" (115).

On one hand, Hébert's Satanic figure incarnates otherness – racial or sexual otherness, for example. On the other hand, however, for Hébert, most importantly, the Devil lies within. He is, to cite Wulf Koepke – although he was not speaking of Hébert at all – "the facilitator of secret desires" (159-60). Quoting from Pascal's *Pensées*, Jean-Ephrem announced to Miguel, "Tu ne me chercherais pas si tu ne m'avais déjà trouvé" (106).[31] One might suppose, on some literal level, that Jean-Ephrem could be referring to Miguel's life with his dysfunctional family. In that case, the dancer could be saying that the adolescent had already known the Devil, in the shape of his parents. I think Hébert had something else in mind. Temptation by the Devil requires a ready and willing participant. Without free will, the Devil cannot exist; this point is underscored by Gérald Messadié (184).

Each of the three major characters of *Un habit de lumière* also represents the writer. Is the writer not, in the creation of characters, similar to Rose-Alba, who wishes to become "moi de plus en plus" (10) by transforming herself into someone else, like Lady Di or Claudia Schiffer? And is Hébert not herself like "le petit Miguel" (Gosselin 9), as she called him in an interview, for whom she felt such deep compassion, in her refusal to accept "les choses telles qu'elles sont,"[32] in her own profound desire for purity and justice? And, finally, is the writer not also a trickster and illusionist, a shape-shifter and a "liar," in speaking, under the name of another, in the first person, for example? Writing enabled Hébert, as Jacques Godbout put it in his recent cinematographic tribute to her, to "dompter

[ses] démons intérieurs."[33] Through a study of one of her diabolical figures, we come closer to following Hébert's counsel, in that film, to "découvrir [ses] propres diables à [soi] . . . et les accepter." For Anne Hébert, in other words, it was *chacun son diable*.

NOTES

1. And, of course, many references point to George Nelson himself as a diabolical figure. I do not pretend to provide a complete survey here but wish merely to give enough examples to show that the figure abounds in Hébert's work. See Pallister for an analysis of *Les Fous de Bassan* in this regard.

2. See Villeneuve, *Dictionnaire* 498; Ashley 79; Russell 217, 262.

3. Reported by Stanford; see 218.

4. The Boivin volumes contain many other examples. Russell (89) discusses an important figure of Quebec's Catholicism, the seventeenth-century nun, Catherine de Saint-Augustin, tempted by the devil at age five and tormented with diabolic enticements for the rest of her life. Hébert mentions her in *Les Enfants du sabbat*, for instance (101).

5. During Franco's regime, the archbishop of Seville made the following comment about the "danses pécheresses" of the city's fair: "danses diaboliques, ravalant notre cité au rang des plus vils quartiers de Paris." Villeneuve, *Dictionnaire* 240.

6. Brandes provides much insight into this cultural background.

7. As I pointed out in some detail in an ACQS paper in October 2000 ("*Un habit de lumière*: vêtement et désir chez Anne Hébert"), I suspect another possible source for the name Pedro Almevida: an ironic allusion to the rebel filmmaker, another Andalusian, Pedro Almodóvar

– just as Rose-Alba's name, as I indicate later in the present essay, transmits great irony. Co-panelist in 2000, Bénédicte Mauguière developed my suggestion in her "All About *Un habit de lumière*: Pedro Almodóvar and Anne Hébert," presented in preliminary form at conferences in May 2001 and October 2002, and later published as "Stratégies de création et subversion des catégories de genre chez Anne Hébert et Pedro Almodóvar," *Cahiers Internationaux de Symbolisme. Théories et pratiques de la création II. La Création au féminin* 107-108-109 (2004): 93-106.

8. Link passim, e.g. 52; Tejirian 172.

9. Johnson passim, e.g. 84; Ashley 59; Link 52; Villeneuve, *Dictionnaire* 165, 678, 942. Russell, for instance, states: "Most earlier [i.e. earlier than Milton] writers describe his deformation at the moment of his fall, and paintings show the bright angels turning into black, twisted shapes as they fall from heaven" (111). See also Fanon 152. G. Etienne's analysis of Blacks in Quebec literature is of considerable relevance here. The Devil is also seen, but less frequently, as red, or even blue.

10. Koepke; Villeneuve, *Dictionnaire* 36, *Beauté* 185. Ashley notes, for example, that he is "said to have seduced both Adam and Eve" (59).

11. Russell 61; Stanford 2, 266. Other animals associated with the Devil, all of which Hébert used in her writing: the black cat, the goat, the fox, and the wolf.

12. Dance is an important metaphor in Hébert's work, from her earliest texts. See my "La Danse chez Anne Hébert: un demi-siècle de corps féminins."

13. Koepke 154-55; Link 56; Tejirian 188.

14. Villeneuve takes the quote from l'Apocalypse de Jean 12.9.

15. Villeneuve, *Dictionnaire* 16. Stanford (66) indicates the expression as a Biblical quote from John 8.44, where Jesus characterizes the Devil: "car il est

menteur et le père du mensonge" ("L'Evangile selon Jean" 8.44).

16. For the trickster, see, in particular: Stanford 187; Mercatante 11; Link 16, and the entire Hynes-Doty volume; Doty's chapter on Hermes is especially rich (46-65). For the roving nature: Russell 120; Forsyth, *Old Enemy* 114. For amorality: Mercatante 11.

17. Lacoste speaks of him as a "Gitan" (417). I find nothing compelling in the text to suggest this reading, although I do agree that Hébert might have been paying homage to Federico García Lorca in the novel.

18. DDASS = Direction Départementale des Affaires Sanitaires et Sociales.

19. In the earlier paper, "*Un habit de lumière*: vêtement et désir chez Anne Hébert," as yet unpublished but submitted for publication, I spoke of some of the parallels with the Marie-Claire Blais novel of the same name. See note 7.

20. I thank Christiane Lahaie, the Director of the Center at the time, for this information transmitted orally during the ACQS meeting in Montreal in 2000.

21. One could argue that Jean-Ephrem's remark about the strangeness of the term "adieu" (117) also underscores the absence of God. Janet Paterson, however, in her foreword to *The Art and Genius of Anne Hébert: Essays on Her Works*, edited by Janis L. Pallister (Madison: Fairleigh Dickinson UP, 2001, 11-13), proposes that the image of "[q]uelqu'un de sacré" (137), seen in the water by Miguel just before his death, carries spiritual promise. Paterson speaks of "an ultimate luminous image of hope, a powerful glimpse of redemption and grace" (13). One could object to the Paterson conclusion that the adjective "sacré" has earlier been used by Jean-Ephrem in reference to himself and to Miguel: "Et tout sera égal entre nous, animal et sacré. Sauf que c'est moi le maître" (67). The closing image of Miguel's life is therefore, at best, ambiguous.

22. ". . . As-tu déjà eu une mère?" asks Miguel. – "Jamais! . . . a-t-il répondu. . . ." (101).

23. Lacoste has written of Michael as the patron saint of Seville (416). That detail seems less significant than Michael's role as the adversary of Lucifer.

24. See p. 42 for "jumeaux." See also p. 26: "Tous deux dans l'extase de soi et de son double. Complices et amoureux."

25. I thank Janis Pallister, the first reader of this article, for her helpful comments, and especially for the reference to the "Litany of the Blessed Virgin Mary." Hébert relates Rose-Alba to the Virgin rather openly on two occasions: "vierge de moi et de [mon père]" (95) and "je redeviens vierge à jamais" (122). There are also mentions of gold, "une petite robe d'or comme un soleil abrégé" (22) and "splendeur dorée" (48), as well as stars, "ma robe de velours noir, criblé d'étoiles brillantes" (31) and "une vraie star" (51). Other ironic echoes of ideal maternity in Rose-Alba's name: Roseanna Lacasse of *Bonheur d'occasion* or Rosa Gaudrault of *Le Premier jardin*. A further source for the name may be a saint, Rose de Lima, referred to in an earlier Hébert text, *Les Enfants du sabbat* (e.g. 140). The Peruvian saint's desire was to destroy her physical beauty and to reject the material world. Coulson, especially, gives a good summary of her characteristics.

26. The allusion to the tale of *Peau d'âne* (26), with the father's incestuous attraction to his daughter, supports Hébert's insistence on little Miguel's joy at sleeping with his mother (42, 45), reinforcing this aspect of the intimacy between mother and son.

27. As I wrote in my "Marie-Josephte Becomes Ludivine: The Family Reformed in Anne Hébert's *La Cage*," "Like other writers of Quebec, Anne Hébert mines – and undermines – the image of the Holy Family" (27).

28. Werblowsky quotes Wilson Knight's point that "Michael has to cut a rather poor figure . . . because 'nothing less than the Messiah can prove victor over [Satan's] heroic virility'" (98). Russell speaks of a "stalemate" (105) between Satan's armies and those of Michael.

29. I discuss the significance of clothing in this novel in the article referred to in note 19.

30. There is, of course, a vast difference in the reader's understanding of Irène and Miguel because the latter has a voice in the novel, whereas the former remains imprisoned in her silence.

31. VII, 553, p. 148, in a relatively lengthy passage entitled "Les Mystères de Jésus," a meditation on the suffering of Christ. Jean-Ephrem leaves out the first two words, "Console-toi," and adds a "déjà" not present in the Pascal text.

32. I quote from the Jacques Godbout film.

33. J. Godbout was, of course, referring to the title of the 1982 Claude Godbout film on Hébert in the "Profession écrivain" series: *Anne Hébert: Dompter les démons.*

WORKS CITED

Ashley, Leonard N. *The Complete Book of Devils and Demons*. New York: Barricade, 1996.

Blais, Marie-Claire. *La Belle Bête*. Montréal: Pierre Tissayre, 1968.

Boivin, Aurélien. *Le Conte fantastique québécois au dix-neuvième siècle*. Montréal: Fides, 1987.

——. *Les Meilleurs contes fantastiques québécois du dix-neuvième siècle*. Québec: Fides, 2001.

Brandes, Stanley H. *Metaphors of Masculinity: Sex and Status in Andalusian Folklore*. Philadelphia: U of Pennsylvania P, 1980.

Buttrick, George Arthur. *The Interpreter's Dictionary of the Bible: An Illustrated Encyclopedia*. New York: Abingdon, 1962.

Cooke, Brett, George E. Slusser, and Jaume Marti-Olivella, ed. *Critical Studies: The Fantastic Other, an Interface of Perspectives*. Amsterdam: Rodopi, 1998.

Coulson, John. *The Saints: A Concise Biographical Dictionary*. New York: Hawthorne, 1958.

Day, A. Colin. *Roget's Thesaurus of the Bible*. New York: Harper Collins, 1992.

Etienne, Gérard. *La Question raciale et raciste dans le roman québécois: Essai d'anthroposémiologie*. Montréal: Balzac, 1995.

Fanon, Frantz. *Peau noire, masques blancs*. Paris: Seuil, 1952.

Forsyth, Neil. "The Devil in Milton." *Etudes de Lettres* 2. (1989): 79-96.

——. *The Old Enemy: Satan and the Combat Myth*. Princeton: Princeton UP, 1987.

Godbout, Claude. *Anne Hébert: Dompter les démons*. Montréal: Productions Prisma, 1982.

Godbout, Jacques. *Anne Hébert 1916-2000*. Office National du Film du Canada, 2001.

Gosselin, Michel. "Entrevue avec Anne Hébert." *Les Cahiers Anne Hébert* 2: *Anne Hébert et la modernité*. Ville Saint-Laurent: Fides (2000): 5-11.

Hébert, Anne. "L'Ange de Dominique." *Le Torrent*. Ville la Salle: L'Arbre HMH, 1976. 47-75.

——. *Les Enfants du sabbat*. Paris: Seuil, 1975.

——. *Les Fous de Bassan*. Paris: Seuil, 1982.

——. *Un habit de lumière*. Paris: Seuil, 1999.

——. *Héloïse*. Paris: Seuil, 1980.

——. *Kamouraska*. Paris: Seuil, 1970.

——. *Le Premier jardin*. Paris: Seuil, 1988.

——. *Le Torrent*. 1950. Ville la Salle: L'Arbre HMH, 1976.

Hynes, William J. and William G. Doty, eds. *Mythical Trickster Figures: Contours, Contexts, and Criticisms*. Tuscaloosa: U Alabama P, 1993.

Ingham, John M. *Mary, Michael, and Lucifer: Folk Catholicism in Central Mexico*. Austin: U Texas P, 1986.

Johnson, Lemuel A. *The Devil, the Gargoyle, and the Buffoon: The Negro as Metaphor in Western Literature*. Port Washington, NY: Kennikat, 1971.

Koepke, Wulf. "Nothing But the Dark Side of Ourselves? The Devil and Aesthetic Nihilism." *Critical Studies: The Fantastic Other, an Interface of Perspectives*. Ed. Brett Cooke, George E. Slusser, and Jaume Marti-Olivella. Amsterdam: Rodopi, 1998. 143-63.

Lacoste, Liliane. "L'Espagne de Lorca revisitée par Anne Hébert dans *Un habit de lumière*." *Francographies* 2.3 (2000): 411-18.

Link, Luther. *The Devil: The Archfiend in Art from the Sixth to the Sixteenth Century*. New York: Henry N. Abrams, 1995.

Mercatante, Anthony S. *Good and Evil: Mythology and Folklore*. New York: Harper and Row, 1978.

Messadié, Gérald. *A History of the Devil*. Trans. Marc Romano. New York: Kodansha, 1996.

Pagels, Elaine. *The Origin of Satan*. New York: Random House, 1995.

Pallister, Janis L. "Satanism, Jansenism and Greek Myth in *Les Fous de Bassan*." *Carrefour de cultures: Mélanges offerts à Jacqueline Leiner.* Dir. Régis Antoine. *Etudes littéraires françaises* 55 (1993): 541-54.

Pascal, Blaise. *Pensées.* Garden City: Doubleday, 1961.

Perrault, Charles. "Peau d'âne." *Contes.* Ed. Marc Soriano. Paris: Flammarion, 1989.

Rea, Annabelle M. "La Danse chez Anne Hébert: un demi-siècle de corps féminins." *The Art and Genius of Anne Hébert: Essays on Her Works.* Ed. Janis L. Pallister. Madison: Fairleigh Dickinson UP, 2001. 251-63.

——. "Marie-Josephte Becomes Ludivine: The Family Reformed in Anne Hébert's *La Cage.*" *Doing Gender: Franco-Canadian Women Writers of the 1990s.* Eds. Roseanna L. Dufault and Paula Ruth Gilbert. Madison: Fairleigh Dickinson UP, 2001. 23-35.

Roy, Gabrielle. *Bonheur d'occasion.* 1945. Montréal: Stanké, 1977.

Russell, Jeffrey Burton. *Mephistopheles: The Devil in the Modern World.* Ithaca: Cornell UP, 1986.

Serrin, Phyllis M. "The World, the Flesh, and the Devil: The Crusade of Lionel Groulx 1878-1967." Diss. York U, 1975.

Stanford, Peter. *The Devil: A Biography.* New York: Holt, 1996.

Storms, Colette. "Le Mal dans Philomena." *Imaginaires du mal.* Dir. Watthee-Delmotte, Myriam et Paul-Augustin Deproost. Paris: Editions du Cerf, 2000. 103-13.

Tejirian, Edward J. *Sexuality and the Devil: Symbols of Love, Power, and Fear in Male Psychology.* New York: Routledge, 1990.

Villeneuve, Roland. *La Beauté du diable.* Paris: Bordas, 1994.

——. *Le Diable. Erotologie de Satan.* Paris: Jean-Jacques Pauvert, 1963.

——. *Dictionnaire du diable.* Paris: Omnibus, 1998.

Watthee-Delmotte, Myriam et Paul-Augustin Deproost, dir. *Imaginaires du mal.* Paris: Editions du Cerf, 2000.

Werblowsky, Raphael Jehudah Zwi. *Lucifer and Prometheus: A Study of Milton's Satan*. London: Routledge and Kegan Paul, 1952.

Transgendered Identities in Anne Hébert's *Un habit de lumière* and Almódovar's *All About My Mother*

BÉNÉDICTE MAUGUIÈRE

Anne Hébert, "la grande dame de la littérature québé-coise," and Pedro Almódovar, the child prodigy of the Spanish cinema, are apparently so different that it could seem strange to compare them.[1] However, their works present many common thematic and aesthetic points: the same obsessions, life as a theater play, the excesses of passion and desire, the fascination of death, and most importantly, common strategies of creation. The desire to escape from all absolute thought comes as a result of their education in tradi-tional and repressive societies dominated by the Catholic clergy, the *Duplessisme* in Quebec *("La Grande Noirceur")* in Hébert's case and *Franquisme* for Almódovar. Their writings are a response, a kind of undoing of the Manichean "black and white" dual-ism of order and disorder identified with Good and Evil they try hard to deconstruct to go back to an orig-inal purity before the fall.[2] Their works reject in a rad-ical way the symbolical Order of the Father and claim a speech that openly inspires "les lieux prélogiques de la mémoire" (Lejeune). In this perspective, it is about thinking against mainstream ideas, through strategies labeled as excessive, in a sort of going back to the origins.

Androgyny

For Almódovar, in *All About My Mother*, going back to the origin of the world allows the transsexual to reclaim his divine essence, the primitive androgyny, man and woman simultaneously. Similarly, the transvestite character in the novel *Un habit de lumière* by Anne Hébert is searching to achieve perfection in his "suit of light." The loss of paradise is, in effect, always present:

> Le paradis terrestre existe réellement dans notre mémoire génétique et il arrive que, le temps d'un éclair mental, on s'en souvienne (...). Ce paradis de la fratrie prénatale, nous souffrons inconsolablement de sa perte, comme d'un vertigineux trou de mémoire, un tourment infernal. (Lejeune 19)

Therefore it is not surprising that this place is called "Le Paradis perdu" in Hébert's book and that the main character kills himself from the despair of not being able to go back there (75).[3] The fact that Almódovar's characters in *All About My Mother* are transsexuals and not transvestites as in Hébert's novel is not unusual given the fact they manage to get to the root of this suffering and transcend it. They did achieve the metamorphosis that the hébertian characters also strive for, without ever reaching it, due to the fact that their metamorphosis remains a travesty, an illusion.

I will begin by identifying the common strategies of creation of these two authors, and then demonstrate that the objective of these strategies is to subvert the gender categories in both Hébert's *Un habit de lumière* and in the screen play of Almódovar's *All About My Mother* (the two works were released in 1999). Regarding the strategy of creation, it is defined here as the wish to distort and to deconstruct oppressive binary gender categories. I will keep, without a pre-established order, four elements that seem to me fundamental to this strategy: intertextuality, the choice of a baroque aesthetic (the show, the metamorphosis), the mise en abyme and the choice of a transvestite and of a transsexual as main characters (who sometimes also correspond to the necessity of creating a twin, a double for the author).

In a recent interview with respect to his work Almódovar openly claims the desire of a double when he says: "I desperately need to find a twin soul" (Almódovar, *NYT* 70). Actually, the feminine desire of the brother-man and the masculine desire of the sister-woman are "bien plus biologiquement enraciné dans la nature humaine que le désir oedipien du père et de la mère":

> Dans l'existence prénatale, le masculin et le féminin se connaissent l'un l'autre comme frères et soeurs jumeaux, vitalement branchés l'un sur l'autre, interférents, interactifs, coopératifs. (Lejeune 10)

It is not surprising, then, that Hébert had chosen a

masculine subject and Almódovar, a feminine subject. In a previous study, I demonstrated how a creation of the double is for the woman who writes a strategy of survival destined to subvert the conventions of what is not socially "acceptable" and this creation is also self-censorship (Mauguière 1037).

Intertextuality

According to Janet Paterson, intertextuality is "le désir d'explorer, par la voie d'une parole mobile et plurielle, de nouveaux horizons" (75). Almódovar openly claims the intertextual process and admits that his films are tributes to those who have influenced him, as shown by the long list of films and actresses, to which *All About My Mother* is dedicated (including the title *All About Eve* from which he borrowed). Anne Hébert, by contrast has always been discreet about her influences. This is all the more interesting since her texts are profoundly interlaced by other writings and intertextual references and that an attentive examination shows her text strikingly resonates Almódovar's screen writing. It seems however difficult for her to acknowledge the use of intertextuality as a writing strategy (Mauguière, "L'Auteur"). *Un habit de lumière* does however er directly reference *Paradise Lost*; the name of the club where Miguel meets his Angel. While intertextuality plays an important role in both works, it is intrinsically linked with the other elements which will be addressed below.

The World as a Show

For Hébert, "le monde est une scène" and her work is dominated by the fascination for the magic of theater, this art of the artificial and of the show that rests on the talents of actors. Hébert opens her novel *Le Premier jardin* with Shakespeare's quote echoing the sentiment. As the world is a show, gender identity is equally a show, sexuality being represented by the artifice of clothing. Almódovar explains that he was brought up in the La Mancha region in Spain, the cradle of Machismo. This origin profoundly left a mark on him because he tells us that "devant ces hommes qui se prenaient pour des demi-dieux, les femmes devaient trouver des stratégies de survie":

> Against this Manchegan machismo which I remember (perhaps enlarged) from my childhood, the women faked, lied, hid, and that way allowed life to flow, without men finding out or obstructing it. (Aside from being vital, this was quite spectacular.) (Almódovar, *All About My Mother*)

Without knowing precisely at what moment, he decided that this capacity of women to make believe and play a role would be the subject of his film. In fact the film deals with, in the scenes of everyday life, the codes of social, sexual, and emotional representation in which each plays his/her role(s). The very structure of the film and the novel can be compared since, according to Almódovar, *All About my Mother* could be defined as "a delirious drama full of extravagant characters" (Almódovar). In the film, he adds, "each of the elements seems to come from an awfully kitsch novel. And yet, the film, is just the contrary," in contrast with this disproportionate nature, performances are as simple as possible (Almódovar website). Each of these comments is also true for *Un habit de lumière* in which each element taken separately is a genuine caricature while the ensemble contradicts this impression. The writing in particular is minimalist in contrast to the theatrical excesses. Writing is for them an outlet that allows passion to flow freely. The texts have so many similarities that the titles could even be switched. Like Estebàn, the teenager who from the first images of the film wants to write about his mother, all of *Un habit de lumière* (a reference also taken from the macho world of the Spanish bull fight) seems to have been written by Miguel as a tribute to his mother.

Mise en abyme

Mise en abyme is a technique used by the two authors, however more explicitly used by Almódovar. In *All About My Mother*, Manuela's adolescent son, Estebán, is interested in literature and wants to be a writer. He is writing a story about his mother. One of the first scenes of the film shows him watching the film *All About Eve* on television. Watching the film, Estebàn finds his title and writes it in his notebook that he takes everywhere. It is also how the director found the title of the story, *All About My Mother*. Then his mother reads to him the first lines of Truman Capote's text of the fitting title, *Music for Chameleons*: "When God offers you a gift, He also gives you a whip; the usage of the whip is intended solely for self-punishment" (Almódovar, *Tout sur ma mère* 15).

Mother and son go to the theater to see a representation of *A Streetcar Named Desire*, the play by Tennessee Williams (both share a great admiration for Huma Rojo, the actress who plays the part of Blanche Dubois). It is pouring rain but Estebàn wants Huma Rojo's autograph. Waiting for the actress to leave, Manuela confides in her son that 20 years ago, she had played the role of Stella in an amateur group with his father who had played the role of Stanley Kowalski and that is how they had met one another. Estebàn is surprised by this unexpected confidence because his father, whom he had always wanted to meet, had never been mentioned before this moment. Shortly thereafter, Huma Rojo and Nina Cruz, the actress who plays Stella, leave from the artists' entrance and rush into a taxi. Estebàn follows them under the battering rain, is hit by a car and dies. The names Rojo (Red) and Cruz (Cross) here have a notable symbolism.

The theme of the fan who ends up dying because of his admiration for the theater world and/or the actor or actress who embodies it is a favored theme by Almódovar.[4] This is also the theme of *Un habit de lumière* and perhaps Hébert drew her inspiration from the Almódovar name to create the family name Almevida (also considering, of course, the play on words with *A mi vida / A ma vie*). The following passage from *Un habit de lumière* could have been written for the most tragic scene of the film described above in the course of which the young Estebàn dies, having been thrown onto the windshield of a car at night because of the rain:

> Ça brille et ça miroite en bas, sur l'asphalte, à cause de la pluie. Toutes ces voitures vont quelque part, c'est certain, chacune avec (...) son essuie-glace qui bat comme un coeur en larmes contre le pare-brise. Attention ça dérape (...). Voitures tordues. Ambulances, police et pompiers, sirènes hurlantes. Bientôt, il s'agira de faire le compte de la nuit qui s'achève et de départager les morts d'avec les vivants, tandis que l'aube tombera sur la ville comme une bruine d'argent, à cause de la pluie. (Hébert 86)

In his acceptance speech for the Oscar for best foreign film, Almódovar mentions the three films that moved him the most, being *Opening Night, All About Eve* and *The Important Thing Is to Love*: "The spirit of these films impregnates the characters in *All About My Mother* with smoke, alcohol, desperation, madness, desire, frustration, solitude, vitality, and understanding." All these elements are also at the heart of *Un habit de lumière*. However, if Almódovar purposefully inserts a tribute to Tennessee Williams by integrating *A Streetcar Named Desire* in the film so that he makes the play an integral part of the film, Hébert uses all these elements but leaves the reader to identify them. The only character that can be easily identified is

Pedro, the caricature of the machismo that Almódovar had in mind when he made his film.[5] This character is returned to the animal kingdom and repeatedly compared to a bull: "lui-même taureau, mon père, respirant fort dans sa fureur" (Hébert 41). The loving relationship is for them like a fight in the arena,[6] a conquest, a submission to the other. Pedro is compared to a "seigneur qui revient de la guerre," by contrast, her son, Miguel is called, "Petite bête" that recalls the "l'animalité innocente."[7]

Choices of characters and figures of redemption

Un habit de lumière contains numerous references to the figure of the matador. Several times Rose-Alba compares her son to a bullfighter in the middle of the arena: "L'odeur du sang et de la mort me poursuit" (Hébert 10). This bloody theater is dominated by the colors of red and black, like the bullfighter's cape and Jean-Ephrem de la Tour's "chateau rouge et noir" (Hébert 89). The two works are dominated by desire and death through which the characters chase a black Angel in a suit of light. In *All About My Mother,* Manuela follows the transsexual Lola, her son's father who seduced her adoptive daughter, Rosa. It is ironic to note that, in *Un habit de lumière*, mother and son are seduced by a transvestite disguised as an Angel, who is black, as in *All About My Mother*, mother and son are seduced by the black Angel. In *All About My Mother*, Manuela plays the role of the saving Angel and in *Un habit de lumière*, it is Miguel who plays the role of St. Michel. All have this same desire of sacrifice and salvation sometimes despite themselves:

> Je suis si lourd, si lourd, pareil à une femme qui porte son enfant sur le dos. Jean-Ephrem de la Tour, mon mari. Je le délivrerai de son mal. Je prendrai son fardeau à ma charge, attaché à moi comme une grosse pierre pour me noyer. (Hébert 136)

Miguel, the expiatory victim in *Un habit de lumière*, echoes Truman Capote's sentence on self-punishment when he talks about his father:

> Il ne faut pas qu'il sache que je saute à la corde à la récré comme une fille, malgré sa défense. La nuit, je fais un rêve. [...] Il y a une corde à sauter qui vient du plafond contre le mur. Elle se déroule toute seule vers le bas, tout doucement, comme un serpent qui descend. Je sais qu'on doit me battre avec cette corde, que c'est pour ça qu'elle vient vers moi. Je me couche par terre. (Hébert 56)

The father here is compared to God-the-Father in the Spanish machismo tradition of Almódovar's childhood and he is in charge of punishing Miguel's sexual ambivalence. Therefore we understand why Miguel is also desperate to escape from this oppressing patriarchal tradition and is so seduced by the androgynous character of the Paradis Perdu who seems to be the only one in a position to validate his existence. It is through images of death and redemption that Almódovar makes us go back to the Paradis Perdu while this return for Hébert is symbolically and literally unattainable. If religion, and more precisely Catholicism, with its punitive procession, is very present in the texts of the two authors, Almódovar's characters transcend it by their humanity while Hébert's characters always seem to struggle with guilt. From these two authors, the bisexual characters are like appearances and have an almost mythic quality as in the astonishing scene of "l'apparition de Lola" in *All About My Mother*, or the fantastic one of Hébert's Jean-Ephrem who incarnates "l'univers magique tout entier" (Hébert 75). However, if Almódovar deconstructs the gender categories with irony, then there is neither a future nor a return possible in Hébert's text because she shows the oppressive character of the binary categories but she does not succeed in surpassing them. While at the end of the text, the Order of the Father continues to reign more than ever with Miguel's suicide and the return of his father Pedro who prowls the city, Almódovar settles his issues with machismo by rewriting the last lines of *A Streetcar Named Desire* and by symbolically reinventing the scene where Stella leaves Stanley Kowalski with her baby: "I will never come back to this house" (Almódovar, *Tout sur ma mère* 87). By rewriting the end of a classic piece, he inserts reality into fiction and shows Manuela's awareness, the ability to control her destiny as a subject. At the end, she says these words to her son: "I could have been an actress, but I chose to raise you instead," thus banishing a tormented destiny and turning her back on the world of appearances and of theater to which she prefers real life.

To the linear mind of the macho man, Almódovar opposes men and women who defy the codes of sexual representation, while the hébertian character is not successful in escaping them. Rose-Alba's destiny drives her to choose the world of appearances instead of real life and she could have said to her son, Miguel, the inverse of Manuela's sentence: "I could have raised you but I chose to be an actress instead." Thus, Miguel's mimicking desire toward Jean-Ephrem is condemned, and he dies. If the scene direction and the world of appearances is the cause of death for the two teenagers, it is a voluntary death only in the novel. In the two cases, it is caused at night by the water, evoking the origins of the primal world to birth. The gender representations are pushed to the limits in as much by Hébert as by Almódovar since in one case, Miguel loves a transvestite who is equally desired by his mother and in the other case, Esteban, who is the son of a transsexual, is attracted to an actress who is romantically involved with another woman.

Theatre and Baroque Aesthetics

Hébert and Almódovar also have in common baroque aesthetics. Baroque literary works are characterized by a refusal of classic linear narration, a tendency for a multi-layered framework, and thematical inconsistency, games between the illusion and disillusion. Two major baroque traits appear in the narrative: metamorphosis and ostentation. Ostentation refers to excess, its spectacular side, its tendency to favor appearances to the detriment of the being. The same narrative strategy is used by Hébert and Almódovar since each chose the representation as a show by way of the theater which is at the center of both the novel and the film and is an integrated part, so much so that they can no longer be distinguished from one another. If baroque is in itself a theatrical attitude in life, the final scene between Jean-Ephrem and Miguel at the end of *Un habit de lumière* is particularly troubling:

– J'aurais tant voulu être une fille et me marier avec toi. Je lui parle de robe de mariée, blanche et mousseuse jusque par terre. (...) Je lui débite la formule consacrée du mariage.
– . . . Oui, oui, je veux bien tout cela, me marier avec toi.
– . . . Parler dans le noir de mes paupières baissées. Me laisser aller à des répliques de théâtre dignes du Paradis perdu.(...)Je le pousse vers la porte. Je lui dis adieu tendrement, *comme dans les romans*. (Hébert 135)

Given that Almódovar's first intention was to make a film on the abilities of some people who are not actors to play a role, the first lines of *Un habit de lumière* are better understood when they are put into perspective with Almódovar's fascination for the dressing room. According to him the dressing room is the place where REAL LIFE happens and he adds that: "When she puts on make-up, it's the moment in which the actress does not lie" (Almódovar website). The *All About Eve* scene that Estebán watches on television in the beginning of the film is the one which takes place in the actress's dressing room. Another significant scene takes place in Huma Rojo's dressing room, in front of a mirror.[8] The theme of the dressing room resonates in a similar way in Hébert's first lines of *Un habit de lumière* where she plays on the two meanings of the word "*loge*" (dressing room) in French, one pertaining to the concierge and the other pertaining to the theater that Rosa-Alba confuses in her mind:

> C'est moi qu'on voit par la fenêtre grande ouverte de la loge. Côté rue. Moi, accoudée, qui prends l'air. Ma tête, mes cheveux, ma face adorée, mes épaules rondes, ma forte poitrine, mon peignoir de satin rose, tout ce que j'ai de plus beau, je le montre par la fenêtre. Je fais voir mon haut, tout habillé, pour les passants. (Hébert 9)

The theater being the art of ostentation, what better definition of excess, of appearance? Ostentation is also a strategy of seduction since one wants to parade to make oneself loved like in Algrado's remark ("celui qui veut plaire") in his live monologue when he details how much each surgery cost him, in a sentence which seems to have been custom written for the character Rose-Alba Almevida:

> It cost me a lot to be authentic. But we must not be cheap in regards to the way we look. Because a woman is more authentic the more she looks like what she has dreamed for herself. (Almódovar, *All About My Mother*)

Metamorphosis

This ironic commentary evokes Rose-Alba Almevida's scene at the hairdresser's that she describes as: "L'opération terminée se dresse devant moi dans la glace une créature éclatante et dorée qui se prétend moi. Je file doux et je n'ose la contredire. Toute à ma contemplation infinie" (Hébert 49). Here the metamorphosis intervenes. The entire novel is centered on this process of metamorphosis, that of Jean-Ephrem, of Miguel, and especially of Rose-Alba, who, by revelation of Jean-Ephrem's "l'univers magique," makes the appearances coincide with "le fond d'elle-même, là où tout est rêve et splendeur":

> Je m'abîme en silence dans des envies furieuses d'hôtel quatre étoiles, de voitures de maître avec chauffeur en livrée, de fards lumineux, de crèmes onctueuses, de mascaras indélébiles, de vins millésimés, de fourrures, de fourrures surtout, renards roux ou argentés, panthères ocellées, douces zibelines, afin que je sois à tout jamais changée en bête splendide et féroce, faite pour l'amour et pour le sacre. (Hébert 11-12)

Miguel himself is fascinated by the illusion created by his mother's metamorphosis and the universe of fairy tales that she evokes. Talking about her dress, he says: "Aucune reine ou actrice célèbre n'en ont de pareille. [. . .]Peau d'Ane n'a qu'à bien se tenir" (Hébert 26).

This metamorphosis finds its climatic point in Jean-Ephrem de la Tour's dance scene in the Paradis

Perdu, supreme theatrical celebration, baroque celebration with "ses merveilles" to the limits of outrageousness (Hébert 75). The whole show becomes an effective seduction apparatus of the mother as well as the son and Jean-Ephrem admits that when he speaks about the Paradis Perdu to Miguel, "la séduction fait son chemin" (Hébert 63). This place is by definition the one of metamorphosis, the place of the "mutation d'anges ou de démons"(Hébert 67). Rose-Alba puts herself in the first row and imagines that the scene is for her:

> C'est là que je suis la plus heureuse, parmi des créatures de rêve, parées comme des chapelles, jetées toutes vives dans la fournaise, au son d'une musique fracassante. (Hébert 91)

and she adds:

> J'aime plus que jamais qu'on crucifie par les ailes Jean-Ephrem de la Tour avant de la lâcher sur scène comme un grand papillon noir, toutes ailes battantes. (Hébert 111)

Jean-Ephrem compares himself to a moth "Ailes d'argent accrochées aux épaules" (61), "C'est moi, là, plumes déployées, cloué au mur par les ailes, comme une chouette sur une porte de grange"(Hébert 87). Further in the text, he is compared to "un roi nègre dans son château rouge et noir" (89), his residence similar to theater decor, "le lit immense sur une estrade, la mousseline blanche en baldaquin" (Hébert 85). He is undeniably a predator, compared to a wolf "aux dents excessivement blanches et fortes," "la bouche sanglante" (Hébert 63, 66). The theme of possession is recurring, that of the vampire that nourishes himself from his victim, makes a clean sweep and then begins again with another prey: "(...)je suis fait pour vivre, (...)vivre sans scrupules, tu comprends? (...)Je n'ai plus qu'une idée en tête à présent, recommencer à vivre comme si de rien n'était" (Hébert 132, 135).

This couple, composed of a savior and a destructive personality, also describes Huma Rojos and Nina Cruz, junkie without scruples, who is utterly the cross of the actress for whom she is "comme une drogue". The main colors are red and black and they each dream of an image. Huma says to Manuela: "I began to smoke to imitate Bette Davis, now, I smoke like a chimney"(Almódovar, *All About My Mother*). The smoke also completely saturates the atmosphere of *Un habit de lumière,* be it at home or at the Lost Paradise: "Je mange dans la fumée, je bois dans la fumée, je respire la fumée d'après l'amour" (Hébert 18):

> Lorsque je sors dans la rue je respire la fumée sur moi comme si j'étais mon père lui-même tout fumant. J'ai l'air de quelqu'un qui se promène avec cent cigarettes dans la bouche. Je suis empesté. (Hébert 55)

The smoke symbolizes what masks and deforms reality, the illusion for these people of the mirror who live through the reflection of the other as Miguel states it:

> Ce que je vois a de quoi me surprendre, mais je reconnais aussitôt ma véritable image, qui vient à ma rencontre, superbe et innocente dans la glace. Je lui souris

tendrement et mon image répond, également tendre et souriante, image, image, belle image de moi, Miguel Almevida. (Hébert 107)

[...] J'articule nettement, comme dans une pièce de théâtre où j'aurais un rôle et où je ne serais pas là pour de vrai. (Hébert 130)

The pejorative connotations of the theatricality seen as a metaphor of an inauthentic world are evident here. The baroque breaks down the barriers between reality and illusion and the ostentation refers to the meta-morphosis. As we have seen, the fact of bringing the stereotypes to their limit is a strategy of creation that pushes the notions of gender identity. It also brings into the light the social hypocrisy and allows the going back to the origin of the Lost Paradise. Therefore, when Miguel says to Jean-Ephrem: "j'ai toujours voulu être une fille et qu'on m'a persécuté pour cela," he responds to Miguel:

Souviens-toi, dans le ventre de ta mère, tu as déjà été fille et garçon à la fois, un tout petit instant avant le choix insensé d'être un garçon seulement. (Hébert 106)

However, the world being a vast scene, no desire comes without a price and Miguel hardly believes in Jean-Ephrem's drama yet he can not help being drawn into it: "Rire de sa noblesse de théâtre. L'adorer comme un Dieu ravageur et cruel" (Hébert 115). Con-trary to Almódovar's characters, Miguel is unable to resemble what he dreamt of being and he dies from not being able to become "authentic". His mother,

Rose-Alba, does not come to realize either her dream of being an actress or her stereotypical femininity that she never questions. If the choice of the character indicates a strategy of creation, it would seem that it would be more difficult for a woman who writes to escape exterior models of femininity and to be an object of desire. This research leads to a kind of "inauthenticity," of cross dressing the gender identity. Paradoxically, it is the transsexual character in Almódovar who is a success because he himself is fully "authentic." He can play on the fact that since it is the clothing that marks the sexual identity, he can make appearances correspond to reality. This gender identity is chosen and not imposed by artificial exterior criteria. Not only does he succeed in completely fulfilling his gender identity but he also creates life at the end of the film with the birth of a child. In as much as Almódovar like Hébert uses the same strategies of creation, the result is however very different.

In her work, Judith Butler shows that gender behavior is not the result of a pre-established identity. According to her, there is not a gender identity above and beyond the expressions of identity. Identity is constituted by the "expressions," even those that are supposed to be its markers. Identity is then considered a *significant practice*, the gender categories being defined in a constitutive way by what we "do" and like all significant practice, it depends upon the repetition of words and actions. Butler also attracts the attention to the fact that the favored model to subvert cultural gender categories is the parodical expression of these same categories. This process reveals the illusion that gender identity is innate. The loss of norms leads then to an effect of *proliferation* of gender configurations, of destabilizing the fixed male/female identities and of compulsory heterosexuality of the main characters as seen in Judith Butler's works.[9] Almódovar inscribes himself in this "aesthetics of transgression" practiced by Oscar Wilde and the modalities of this transcription are what differentiate Almódovar from Hébert:

> Wilde's experience of deviant desire . . .leads him not to escape the repressive ordering of society, but to a re-inscription within it, and an inversion of the binaries upon which that ordering depends. (Dollimore 248)

When facing the gender categories as an analytical perspective of literary creation, it is particularly interesting to see how "gay creation" modifies and completely subverts these categories. The fact that literary criticism continues to envision them through the traditional polarity of male/female is now insufficient. As we have seen, Hébert seems to impose self-censorship mechanisms upon herself while Almódovar asserts this subversion. For me this is why it seems important for all reflections on gender categories to integrate a "gay" perspective because, with the disappearance of the male/female polarization, it is indeed the "tyrannie de l'identité de genre" that is disappearing. This comparative perspective is the best at bringing into the light the fact that self-censorship continues to dominate female creativity. To explore the male/female strategies of creation, it would be necessary to take into consideration what literary criticism and Queer Theory[10] bring to the debate since the question of gender identity is at the center of their discussions.

NOTES

1. This article is a revised translation of "Stratégies de création et subversion des catégories de genre chez Anne Hébert et Pedro Almodovar". Cahiers internationaux de symbolisme. Belgium: Université de Mons 107-108-109 (2004-2005): 93-106. Translated by Anna Burns.
2. It is equally significant that both are marginalized with respect to the dominating values and the discourse of a patriarchal society as a result of their choice of life.
3. Already in *Le premier jardin*, Raphael says that "il ne voulait pas ressembler à Eric dans sa nostalgie du paradis perdu" p. 75.
4. See the theme of "Opening Night" with Gena Rowlands to whom the film is dedicated.
5. One also recognizes the figure of *A Streetcar Named Desire*, Stanley Kowalski, who belongs as much in the literary domain as in cinematography.
6. One can see here a play on words between arena and queen (*l'arène et la reine*) (that designates the transvestites or "Drag Queens")
7. It is also the term with which Almódovar designates Antonio Banderas in his films.
8. Almódovar always says that actresses talk to him through the mirror.
9. See Judith Butler's works, more specifically: *Bodies that Matter: On the discursive limits of "Sex"* and also *Gender Trouble: Feminism and the Subversion of Identity*.
10. This concept was developed in the American universities with the creation of programs in "Gay and Gender Studies." See the of Yale French Studies n. 90 entitled "Same Sex, Different Text?: Gay and Lesbian writing in French." Yale University, 1996.

All About My Mother. Dir. Pedro Almódovar. Sony Pictures Classics, 2000.

Almódovar, Pedro. Interview. *All About My Mother*. Sony Pictures Classics, 2000.

——. Oscar Speech. Los Angeles, 1999.

——. *Tout sur ma mère*. Bilingual scenario. Trans. Marie Delporte. Paris: Cahiers du Cinema, 1999.

——. *New York Times*. 4 Sept. 2004, 70.

Dollimore, Jonathan. *Sexual Dissidence: Augustine to Wilde, Freud to Foucault*. Oxford: The Clarendon Press, 1991.

Hébert, Anne. *Un habit de lumière*. Paris: Seuil, 1999.

Lejeune, Claire. "L'essai poétique comme espace d'auto-génération." Paper presented at the conference Littératures de langue française: création, recherche et théories critiques. Toronto: York University, 11-14 May 1988.

Mauguière, Bénédicte. "L'homotextualité dans les écritures de femmes au Québec". *The French Review*. 71.6 (May 1998): 1037.

——. "L'Auteur(e) et ses doubles: à la recherche de "l'Inconnu de la Seine"/scène dans *L'Enfant chargé de Songes*." *Cahiers Anne Hébert*. 4 (Spring 2003). Special Number "Anne Hébert et la critique." Quebec: Fides/Université de Sherbrooke, 115-128.

Paterson, Janet. *Moments postmodernes dans le roman québécois*. Ottawa: University of Ottawa Press, 1990.

PedroAlmódovar.com. Ferca Network. March 2002. http://www.clubcultura.com/clubcine/clubcineastas/almodovar/eng/homeeng.htm

"J'habite la fièvre et la démence, comme mon pays natal"

Love-Triangle as Political Allegory *in* Kamouraska

Lee Skallerup

At the center of Anne Hébert's novel *Kamouraska* is a complex love-triangle involving Elisabeth d'Aulnières, Antoine Tassy and George Nelson, which is influenced by other characters in the novel: Elisabeth's mother and aunts, Aurélie Caron (Elisabeth's servant) and Jérôme Rolland (Elisabeth's second husband). This triangle can be read as a sociopolitical allegory for Quebec's situation during the time of the novel, the mid-nineteenth century. Each character (or group of characters) embodies an historically specific political/social reality. At the center, Elisabeth represents Quebec, with all of the conflicts, choices and eventual betrayals that the province faced before, during and after the Rebellion of 1837-8. She is torn between her husband Tassy, who represents the past, and Nelson, who represents the (false) future. These three, then, are the major characters of the allegory, while the others previously mentioned are secondary, but still important. Elisabeth's mother and aunts embody the societal pressures; Aurélie, the class differences; and

Rolland, the aftermath of the Rebellion. This political reading does not negate a possible feminist reading of the text. In fact, this interpretation actually can facilitate reading the text both ways (political and feminist) simultaneously.

There have been previous attempts to read *Kamouraska* politically. These interpretations have focused either on the political allusions/historical accuracy of the novel (Talbot), or on the role of the English as either Coloniser (Rose, Green) and/or Other (Fortier, Shek, Pelletier, Boudreau). However, the French characters are not often treated in these readings, and when they are, both the major and secondary characters are looked at as either mythical/traditional figures (Raymond, Zecher, Cohen) or illustrations of the feminine condition (Pascal-Smith). This paper will look at *all* of the major and secondary characters and their role within the structure of the political allegory.

Let us begin with a short history lesson, which, as Talbot illustrates, justifies a political reading. The historical era of *Kamouraska* – and the actual historical love triangle and murder – is that of the 1837-38 rebellion in Quebec. Throughout the novel, Elisabeth hints at the political turmoil that is happening, that did happen. One of the first instances of this is when a voice calls to her: "Elisabeth d'Aulières, veuve Tassy, souvenez-vous de Saint-Denis and et Saint-Eustache!" (Hébert 44). Saint-Denis, Talbot reminds us, is the one battle that the Patriots won. On the other hand, Saint-Eustache represents the most horrific loss that the Patriots suffered, with a number of the French fighters, including their leader, killed in a Church set ablaze by the English General *(Les Patriots)*. More evidence in support of the fact that Elisabeth was aware of the politics of the time is when she exclaims: "Ce jour-là entre tous" (Hébert 202). The day in question is January 31st 1839, the day George killed her husband, and the day that Lord Durham signed his report (Talbot 198).[1] Further, Sorel – one of the major settings for the novel – was one of the historic centers of activity of the Rebellion, with both Patriots and English soldiers constantly passing through. The book also indicates that the general population knew what was going on around them, as illustrated by the testimony of an auberge owner concerning George after the murder: "Tiens-toi donc tranquille, ma femme, parle donc pas tant, peut-être bien qu'il est un officier anglais, il pourrait nous faire prendre; comme on est dans un mauvais règne, il pourrait y avoir eu quelque bataille en haut" (Hébert 217). Although it does not seem to be a major preoccupation of the central and secondary characters of the story, the History of Quebec during that time period plays a role in the narrative.

Antoine Tassy is one of the characters who appears to be unaffected by the Rebellion. One is tempted to ask why, since his power would have been directly threatened. Interestingly enough, it is alluded to in the novel that his mansion was burnt to the ground: "Vous savez bien qu'il n'y a plus rien. Tout a brûlé en 18... Rasé, nu comme la main" (Hébert 74). Note, it is never made clear who set it ablaze: English soldiers or dissatisfied farmers in his seigneurie. But, for a number of reasons our surprise at his lack of concern is misplaced. First, he was the seigneur of Kamouraska, a word that loses its double connotation in the English translation.[2] In French, the word seigneur means not only "the head of a given area of land," but also "God." And Tassy, as a seigneur, was supposedly the god of his land. What does a god care of petty rebellions? Elisabeth's mother reminds us, however: ". . . le Seigneur lui-même me tanne à la longue" (Hébert 53). The gods were beginning to lose their power. Nonetheless, it is still the Seigneur who Mme d'Aulnières is told to take solace in, and it is seigneur Tassy who seduces Elisabeth and offers her a way out of her situation with her mother and aunts: "Mes chères petites tantes, vous ne comprenez rien. Et moi j'aime la chasse. Et j'irai à la chasse . . . Il n'est pas d'ici. Il vient du bas du fleuve. Je ne sais rien de lui. Mais c'est un voyou, j'en suis sûre. De bonne famille, mais un voyou quand-même. Je me ferai respecter de lui, comme une jeune fille à marier" (Hébert 66). But, just as God wasn't the answer for her mother, neither is Tassy the answer for Elisabeth. Very quickly, Elisabeth becomes the victim of Tassy's rage, drunkenness and wandering eye: "Nous sommes vivants, lui et moi! Mariés emsemble. S'affrontant. Se blessant. S'insultant à coeur joie, sous l'oeil perçant de Mme mère Tassy" (Hébert 75).

As it can be seen, the god was falling. Talbot calls it a "degenerate seigneurial class" (Talbot 199). Tassy exemplifies the past that the Rebellion was rebelling against: representative of ancient traditions, Tassy embodies the inability of the old French regime properly to represent and address the problems of the time.

Pelletier calls his death: "[un] sacrifice du dernier représentant d'une race caduque et mis à mort du passé seigneurial révolu" (Pelletier 42). Tassy himself was powerless; his mother was the true bearer of power in the household. Cohen describes Tassy as a sort of Quebecois anti-hero:

> . . . he has no courage, seeing that he seeks to commit suicide. Independence is completely lacking in this weak being who desperately clings to his mother and young wife and who ultimately destroys the balance of nature by hunting, not to nourish himself, but for the pleasure of killing his prey. This ignoble representative of the Ancient Régime reveals the decadence of the dream of the civilization of the New World. (Cohen 136)

Pascale-Smith contends that Tassy's actions and attitude are a result of some deep-seeded "déspoir" (Pascale-Smith 91). His lack of concern about the Rebellion could also be a result of his awareness that his time had passed, that something had to come along to replace him.

And who should come along but Dr. George Nelson. If Tassy represents an antiquated system of religion, class, and inherited power – and, as an extension, language – then Dr. Nelson represents a possible future or at least an alternative: science, education and, of course, English. Symbolically, Tassy and Dr. Nelson had faced off previously; in *collège* the two would square off in games of chess, games that Tassy knew he would not win: "Antoine vous à parler de moi? Il vous a dit qu'au collège nous jouions au échecs, tous les deux? Il aimait perdre, je crois. Avec moi il n'a jamais gagné, pas une seule fois, vous m'entendez?" (Hébert 120). A reminder of the epic rivalry between the French and the English that France was destined to lose? Or, perhaps of the inferiority complex that supposedly plagued Quebec? Dr. Nelson is obsessed with becoming a saint, but a neo-saint for the people of Quebec, one who wants to cast out the past and the tradition, illustrated in his attitude towards the traditional medical practices of the people, particularly Aurélie, who practices a type of superstition on new-borns: "Le pays est infesté de charlatans. L'ignorance, la superstition et la crasse partout. Une honte! Il faudrait empêcher les guérisseurs de tuer les gens. Soigner tout le monde de force! Empêcher votre servante Aurélie de jouer les socières auprès des nouveaunés" (Hébert 118-9). As put by Boudreau:

> Although he selflessly works impossible hours bringing medical care to the poorest and most isolated members of the rural community where he lived, he seeks to liberate them from what he sees as "superstitious" medical practices. In doing so he condemns equally the two traditional purveyors of folk medicine in rural Quebec, the witch and the *ramancheur*. To what extent is this apparent condemnation of "superstitious" medical practice a condemnation of Québécois folk culture? In effect accusing these people of being incapable of attending to their own needs, Nelson's condemnation of the state of medical care in rural Quebec bears a disturbing resemblance to Lord Durham's assessment of the history and literature of the French Canadians. (Boudreau 311)

But his one obsession, his one true goal, is to save Elisabeth from Tassy; a goal juxtaposed with this need to save the people: "Posséder cette femme. Posséder la terre" (Hébert 126). But what were his motivations? Boudreau argues that "[Nelson's] possessiveness suggests that at times he sees Elisabeth as one more trophy to be won from Antoine Tassy" (Boudreau 311). Here we see the ultimate goal of the coloniser, but also the goal of Nelson's quasi-rebellion: power. The questions surrounding his motivations are important since his motivations are tightly interwoven with his role as the outsider – both linguistically and nationally – and they influence how we can read his character in terms of the political allegory.

The fact that Dr. Nelson is English is important. He does, however, hold one major difference over the other English presence in the novel: Nelson has no allegiance to the Queen – he is American. Even though he is clearly an outsider to the community, he is still held in high regard; he is seen by Elisabeth's family as being a "good" thing for her: "Quel bel homme que ce docteur Nelson, si bien élevé et de vieille famille loyaliste américaine. Dommage que la Petite ne l'ait pas rencontré le premier" (Hébert 158). He is physically attractive, as noted during the trial by those testifying (Hébert 201). A suave and seductive English man who is an outsider, and turns out to be a "diable." As outlined by Pelletier:

> Comme Nelson, le Diable apparaît sans prévenir. Il est séduisant, fascinant, beaucoup plus que les simples habitants canadiens-français, diront les jeunes filles. Il parle bien mais peu, ses paroles et sa voix ensorcellent. Il incite à la transgression des lois et des préceptes de la religion catholique…Il s'opposera au prétendant légitime pour

> enlever une femme du clan. Le diable peut aussi se faire
> justicier, punissant celui qui ne respecte pas la loi devine,
> celui qui travaille le dimanche, l'adultère. Aussi George
> Nelson voudra-t-il, en tuant Antoine Tassy, réparer un
> crime resté impuni depuis trop longtemps. (Pelletier 37-8)

Paul Raymond Côté also notes this juxtaposition of
George Nelson as a devil and a self-appointed judge,
stating that: "Nelson se croit lui-même un justicier car
le meurtre d'Antoine Tassy remettra, pense-t-il, les
choses en bon ordre" (Côté 105). Boudreau more generally accuses Nelson of "actively seek[ing] to be an
agent of change" (Boudreau 317). But what good does
this change bring about? Pelletier states: "Il n'aura pas
d'ordre nouveau; justice ne sera pas faite; il n'y aura
pas de retour à l'origine. Rien de ce qui fut rêvé ne
passera dans la réalité" (Pelletier 42).

This is where Nelson becomes more than a symbol
for the English colonisation of Quebec, as suggested
by Boudreau. As Talbot and Côté point out, in the history of the Rebellion there existed historical figures
leading the Patriotes named Nelson. What does this
represent, this use of names from the Rebellion?
Wasn't the Rebellion a rebellion against the Queen
and the colonisation of Quebec? How can a character
who has, on numerous occasions, been associated with
the role of coloniser also be representative of a figure
from the Rebellion? One *Dr.* Robert Nelson both
signed on to create the Republic of Canada, which in
essence forced the French to second-class status within the political system, and fled to the United States –
much like his fictional counterpart. Note here that
both the real and fictional Nelsons *failed* in their

attempts to bring any change. The argument could be made that they in fact *worsened* the situation for those directly affected by their rebellion. Could it be that the author is commenting on the origins of the conflict, a rebellion incited by outsiders, and then deserting the people they sought to free? Seductive, powerful, but ultimately betraying, the Dr. Nelsons couldn't deliver on their promises of freedom and change to those they had led. Even the origins and motivations of the featured rebellions are questionable: the fictional Dr. Nelson was obsessed with not just justice, but also with being able to seize and possess Elisabeth from Tassy. The origin of the *Rebellion des Patriots* was not culture, but money; it was inspired by the American maxim: "No Taxation Without Representation." One could also argue that the real Dr. Nelson's motivation for signing on to create the Republic of Canada was also a question of self-preservation and power. Could it be that Hébert is commenting on the inability of an authentic rebellion to be staged if the instigators are outsiders whose goals are not in the best interest of the group they claim to be liberating?

What makes that reading particularly problematic is that Hébert initially had a more generic name for George Nelson – George Wilson. She only later came across the historical name when her publisher insisted that the name be changed because it was shared by a French actor at the time (Talbot 197). If this change was made *after* the novel was written, can we read this parallel between the historical and fictional Dr. Nelson? Even if we are simply to read the fictional Dr. Nelson as the embodiment of the coloniser, he is a

coloniser who betrays Elisabeth in a way that is different than the Queen does.[3] While the Queen represents
the British colonising power, George – be it Nelson or
Wilson – nonetheless, is an outsider, an American, thus
representing the other major colonising force Quebec
has had to contend with. Nelson or Wilson, the character embodies the stereotype of the American: violent, arrogant, ambitious, and power-hungry. And
because the reasons of his fictional rebellion were not
purely good, ultimately he failed; did the historical
Rebellion fail for a like reason? George Nelson's
nationality is obviously important to the story because,
as Talbot points out, it would be mathematically
impossible and historically implausible for him to be
that young and still be the son of Loyalists (Talbot
200). Still, for the purposes of this allegory, we can
read George Nelson as a colonising presence, but
more specifically as an *American* colonising presence,
importing their ideals, their ways and their attitudes
into the Quebecois landscape. And once the coloniser
has wiped out the old guard (Tassy), Nelson flees,
betraying the person he claimed to have loved and
leaving her with nothing in return. A rebellion is
caused by an external force, not from within the community, and ultimately, it fails. The parallel between
the fictional and historical Nelson simply helps to
solidify this symbolic relationship. At the centre of this
triangle is Elisabeth, our symbol for Quebec. She is
caught between these two powerful influences – Tassy
and Nelson – with all that they represent. But compli-
cating her point of view are the other influences on
both her choices and her perception of her situation.

The most immediate "outside" influences are her aunts and mother. In them, we see the societal pressure of the time. We see in her upbringing the rigidity that was instilled upon her: "Elisabeth, tiens-toi droite! Elisabeth, ne parle pas en mangeant! Elisabeth recommence cette révérence immédiatement! Elisabeth il y a combien de personnes en Dieu? *The cat, the bird*. Le *th* en anglais se prononce la langue sur les dents, n'oublie pas!" (Hébert 54). Note here also the importance that English played in what a "proper" girl was supposed to know. The aunts had a plan for Elisabeth: "Nous éléverons cette enfant. Nous lui apprendrons à lire. Nous lui ferons faire sa première communion. Nous l'amènerons au bal du gouverneur. Nous lui ferrons un grand marriage" (Hébert 47). The plan for Elisabeth is set in stone; it is a plan that her mother concedes, even agrees to: "Il va falloir marier la Petite" (Hébert, 60). The family offers Elisabeth very few choices as to how her life was supposed to be lived, according to class and gender expectations. For Elisabeth, marriage represented an escape from her aunts, but this escape fails. And when she turns to her aunts for help, all they can offer her is another incarnation of the approved status quo, "a brutal patriarchy for an oppressive matriarchy" (Zecher 12). This "oppressive matriarchy" also represents the assimilation of the colonial values embodied in the novel by Queen Victoria, a type of "shared valorisation." As put by Green, "Victoria fittingly represents the might of the British Empire at the height of its power, but as the model of devoted wife and mother of many children, she served to enforce a concept of womanhood – and female sexuality – that was shared by Elisabeth's own French-speaking culture" (Green 961). Her aunts have assimilated a view that seems, if it doesn't come from outside, then it is a view that receives external approval. No wonder English is held up as important when the idealised figure is English. According to Talbot, the mother and aunts stand for "a society whose upper levels – the seigneurial class and the upper middle class particularly – comport themselves in ways that foster obliviousness to national concerns" (Talbot 198). More concerned with social standing than freedom (either personal or national), Elizabeth's mother and aunts try to influence her away from any type of rebellion or freedom, advocating the status quo.

One of the forces or influences that Elisabeth's aunts want to protect her from is Aurélie: "Il faudrait renvoyer Aurélie. Elle a bien mauvaise réputation" (Hébert 43). Here we have a very interesting figure who represents the differences in class within the society. Aurélie is presented at the beginning of the narrative as being a potential escape for Elisabeth: "Aurélie incarne une pulsion de liberté contrainte par la vie étouffante et stérile que mène Elisabeth dans la maison de ses trois tantes" (Côté 106). Ultimately her position is shown as being just as, if not more, precarious than Elisabeth's. Aurélie, at the beginning, is a very strong reminder of the popular part of Quebec history and tradition [4]: "a girl who smokes a pipe, lives with a man she calls her 'uncle,' tells the future with cards, and plays sorceress with the newborns of Sorel" (Zecher 12). Notably, it is this kind of practice that Nelson is trying to rid from society. But as much as Elisabeth looks to Aurélie for advice and as a source of freedom, so too does Aurèlie look at Elisabeth with envy: "Comme vous êtes bien habillée!" (Hébert 63); "Mon Dou que cette robe est jolie! Mon âme pour avoir une comme ça!" (Hébert 133). Essentially, Aurélie does give up her soul for a dress, both literally and symbol- ically. It is with promises of material gain that George manages to convince Aurélie to attempt to kill Tassy. But this opportunity exists because Aurélie essentially abandons her freer ways, those things that represent the parts of Quebec's past that are not favoured by the upper class: "Aurélie ne fréquente plus aucun mauvais garçon. Ne fait plus aucune prophétie sur la vie des nouveau-nés. Elle ne sort plus de tout . . . La dispense de vivre elle-même" (Hébert 169). She has totally embraced the values of the upper class, and when she is presented with a possible way in, she takes it. But the class that she longs to be a part of ultimately betrays her: Elisabeth is released from jail and Aurélie is left to serve the sentence of murder that she didn't even commit. And the upper class conspired to keep her there: "Aurélie Caron . . . C'est une menteuse . . . une débauchée, une ivrognesse, une . . ." (Hébert 46). In the larger context of the political allegory, Aurélie could be seen as representing the lower class that was ultimately betrayed and punished by the upper class leaders of the Rebellion. While most of the leaders fled to the States, most of the lower class that fought as soldiers either died in battles or were hung (as Hébert reminds the reader in the narrative). Aurélie could also represent the willingness of the lower class to abandon its traditions and culture in favour of the promise of economic advancement. Could this again be a critique of the inspiration of the Rebellions? In abandoning her cultural (and class) roots, Aurélie could not escape punishment and instead becomes a scapegoat, someone to place blame upon. Another interesting role that she takes on is the role of a conscience for Elisabeth, a conscience she would rather deny: "Aurélie Caron, Madame s'en souvient-elle? Non, ce n'est pas vrai. Je ne sais de qui vous voulez parler" (Hébert 33). Another dead Patriot for Elisabeth to have to remember, while she simultaneously denies them?

The final influence that tries to act on Elisabeth is her second husband Jérôme Rolland. Jérôme garners the least amount of attention from critics dealing with the novel. What he does represent is what happened *after* the rebellion, both Elisabeth's and Quebec's: the return to "respectability." With nothing left of the promise of the future, Elisabeth turns to the only means of escape that she knows: marriage. She becomes the ideal wife and mother: "Quelle femme admirable vous avez, monsieur Rolland. Huit enfants et une maison si bien tenue . . . Quelle créature dévouée et attentive, une vraie sainte, monsieur Rolland" (Hébert 16). Elisabeth performs this role in order to regain a sense of respectability to herself and to her family. But as pointed out by Zecher, "the Rolland household in Quebec proves to be a prison in a way that those in Sorel and Kamouraska never were" (Zecher 16). Post-Rebellion, Quebec was effectively taken over by the Church, who looked to preserve the respectability and purity of Quebec's people through their doctrine. But, as was revealed through the Quiet Revolution, the Church managed to subject the population of Quebec in its own way. It has been argued that the Church did manage to keep the Quebec culture alive,[5] much like Rolland keeps Elisabeth "alive," but at what cost?

And now we reach the centre of this storm: Elisabeth. Caught between the past and the future, the elite and the popular, Elisabeth is forced to choose, and then deal with the consequences of this choice. Elisabeth's aunts and mother continually referred to her as "la Petite,"[6] which Fortier explains represents "le dénigrement de la femme adulte, indépendante et capable de décisions" (Fortier 68). On a more political framework, this attitude towards Elisabeth reflects the bourgeoisie's belittling attitude towards Quebecois culture in general. Bouchard explains that French-Canadian culture was qualified as "la pauvreté ou la médiocrité (certains allaient jusqu'à dire la vulgarité) . . ." (Bouchard 127). He goes on to explain what kind of effect this attitude would have: "Il en a résulté une incapacité à "nommer le pays," à traduire les expériences américaines (au sens continental toujours) et les véritables sentiments du peuple . . ." (Bouchard 132).

Note both how Elisabeth is denied her real name by her mother and aunts through the nickname, as well as her family's inability, and Elisabeth's own inability, to fully comprehend what was going on around them, both figuratively and literally. Elisabeth is unable or unwilling to tell, or even to understand, her own story – it takes nightmares and haunting visions to make her recount what happened during the time of Rebellion: "Vous entendez des voix, madame Rolland. Vous jouez à attendre des voix. Vous avez des hallucinations. Avez-vous donc tant besoin de distractions qu'il vous faut aller chercher, au plus creux des ténèbres, le fantômes de votre jeunesse?" (Hébert 75). She seemingly is forcing herself to remember, to tell the story, to be able to make sense, to be able to name and give value to that which was forgotten and devalued.

The question of guilt and innocence are two issues that plague Elisabeth's conscience throughout the novel. She is constantly trying to lay her guilt on other characters: Aurélie, Tassy and even Doctor Nelson. As a character and as a class, Aurélie reminds Elisabeth: "Je n'ai jamais été innocente. Ni Madame non plus" (Hébert 61). She also ensures that Elisabeth's own "suffering" is kept in perspective:

> — Deux ans et demi que j'ai été en prison, moi. À cause de vous. À la disposition de la justice, comme ils disent. Tandis que Madame est libre sous caution . . .
> — Deux longs mois de prison, pour moi aussi, Aurélie. Tu oublies cela? [. . .]
> — Je n'oublie rien. Rien de tout. (Hébert 62)

Later on in the novel, when both women are in prison, Elisabeth comments to Aurélie: "J'ai si peur de me salir dans un si mauvais lit, Aurélie, tu sais comme je suis dédaigneuse de toute promiscuité. De toute honte" (Hébert 239-40). We can see just how hypocritical Elisabeth has been towards herself and towards her loyal, lower class servant. Shame is more of an inconvenience to Elisabeth than murder or even the suffering of her companion. She has revealed both her own petty short-sightedness concerning the consequences of her action, of her quasi-rebellion, and her inability to understand how that Rebellion effected those around her.

Her blame is also directed towards her former husband. On more than one occasion Elisabeth attempts to maintain her innocence through the vilification of Tassy: "C'est lui le coupable. Je n'y en suis pour rien. Innocente. Je suis innocente. Humiliée et offensée" (Hébert 82). She also hides behind her beloved Dr. Nelson: "M'exclure de ce jeu de mort, entre Antoine et toi. Innocente! Innocente! Je suis innocente!" (Hébert 229). She equally attempts to hide behind respectability, as Mme Rolland: "Je suis innocente. Mon mari s'appelle Jérôme Rolland et je vais de ce pas lui faire un bout de conduite" (Hébert 92). But by the end, we are shown that this innocence will not save her: "Condamner Elisabeth d'Aulnière au masque froid de l'innocence" (Hébert 233). Elisabeth constantly denies the reality of her role in history. And like all history the lessons of which are not learned, the mistakes are bound to be repeated; much like the past keeps playing and replaying itself in Elisabeth's head. If her innocence and her denial of history does not provide her with any authentic freedom, what, if anything, does? Can a society that denies its history, that denies the reality of its history, ever be free and independent?

Elisabeth is constantly looking for freedom through George Nelson. Their love will free her. Symbolically, the first time Elisabeth mentions the notion of freedom in terms of George Nelson, it's when he uses English: "*Good bye, my love* . . . Comme si tu dis cela, mon amour. On dirait que nous sommes libres, tous les deux" (Hébert 148).

But as the verb tense implies, she is aware of the illusion that their relationship provides, even if she is unwilling to explicitly admit it to herself. Later on in the narrative, Elisabeth begs of her lover:

> Sauvez-moi, docteur Nelson! Sauvez-vous avec moi! Non pas avec des prières et des alchimies vertueuses et abstraites. Mais avec toute votre chair d'homme vivant, avec toute ma chair de femme vivante. Votre nom à donner à votre femme, docteur Nelson, en échange d'un nom exécré. Votre coeur, votre âme à offirir, tout. Un homme à tuer, il le faut. Je suis l'amour et la vie, mon exigence n'a de comparable que l'absolu de la mort (Hébert 167).

Referring to the earlier quote by Bouchard, we see once again the importance of naming, and the inability of Elisabeth to name herself. She is constantly looking to others (Tassy, Nelson) to name her. All action and reactions necessitate an outsider, and these actions and reactions are extreme in nature; she can only understand them and express them in terms of life or death, with no room for compromise. But this approach proves to ultimately lead to her downfall, and her inability to achieve freedom. When Nelson returns from killing Tassy, Elisabeth *dreams* that he says the following words to her: "Voilà, c'est fait. Elisabeth ma femme, tu es libre, à présent. Nous sommes libres, tous les deux . . ." (Hébert 235). But the reality of the situation is far from the dream: "Qui ose répéter le mot 'amour' et le mot 'liberté,' dans l'ombre, sans mourir de désespoir?" (Hébert 237). The result of the Rebellion? Hopelessness. Nelson flees, and leaves Elisabeth to return to the stifling tradition she was looking to break free from. But the tradition has enclosed itself around her, leaving her even less choice than she had when she was younger: hunting, love, Aurélie's company, etc . . . When Jérôme asks his wife on his deathbed, "Elisabeth, tu as eu bien de la chance de m'épouser, n'est-ce pas?" she responds, "Jérôme, sans toi, j'étais libre et je refaisais ma vie, comme on retourne un manteau usé" (Hébert 35-6). Note again here the importance of naming. It is under the guise of Mme Rolland that Elisabeth is trying to hide behind a mask of innocence, of social perfection. But again it is a name that is not her own. The implication of this statement is that without Rolland, she may have finally been able to be Elisabeth d'Aulnières. But the inability of the society – and of Elisabeth – to be able to think in less extreme and rigid terms keeps her from attaining any authentic form of identity – much like Quebec's society, post-Rebellion, had difficulty naming and defining itself in the face of tradition and autocratic rule.

One final element of political allegory in Elisabeth's character lies in her ambiguous attitude towards the English. Ben Z-Shek explains that: "It is as if a struggle were going on within her between the nationalist super-ego, and her anglomanic id, or perhaps the reverse, both basically showing a linguistic and political conflict that is "historical" in the broadest of senses" (Z-Shek 89). Does Nelson, the symbol of the Anglo-American, provide freedom for Elisabeth, or does he condemn her in English the way that the Queen does? Symbolically, the charges against Elisabeth are written in English and are done in the name of the Queen. But as was stated before, Nelson does not represent the British colonising system, but an American one. And the American turns out to be just as devastating as the Queen: *"It is that damned woman that has ruined me"* (Hébert 244). The accusation is made in English, and ends the narrative in much the same way that is began: with the damnation of an English coloniser. More appropriately, it should read, "c'est ce maudit homme qui m'a ruiné." But the fact that Elisabeth is never able to express that thought so coherently speaks volumes about the power of the colonisation.

Marilyn Gaddis Rose states that *Kamouraska* "[exposes] allegorically the colonial mentality prior to national consciousness" (Rose 151), and Elisabeth is the symbol of the results of that colonial mentality. But as pointed out by Gabrielle Pascal-Smith (among others), this novel also reveals the reality of the condition of women. And when looking at the love triangle, set up here as a political allegory, we can also see how Elisabeth could not be only a symbol for Quebec, but also a symbol for the condition of women at that time. All of the other characters discussed here maintain their symbolic influence, but in a personal sense, instead of in a national sense. Thus, Elisabeth embodies the choices, or lack thereof, facing women of that particular period. This is not the first time that

Hébert has used a female character to mirror the situation of Quebec, while commenting simultaneously on the female condition within that society. One needs only to look at one of her most celebrated poems, "Le Tombeau des rois." Published for the first time in the 1950s, early criticism (such as Pierre-Hervé Lemieux) focused exclusively on the national allegory of poem, while later criticism turned its focus to the feminist message of the poem (Patricia Smart). While the poem lends itself to both interpretations simultaneously, no such attempt had been made with *Kamouraska*. Thus, we have seen how the structure of the love triangle is useful, not only in uncovering the political implications of the novel, but in understanding the feminist ones as well.

NOTES

1. The Lord Durham report's goal was to dictate how to "solve" the French-Canadian problem, and concluded that the only way was through assimilation into English. As put by Talbot, "Arguing that French Canadians had no literature and no history, Durham advocated the union of Lower and Upper Canada with the explicit aim of assimilating the French Canadians into a larger and, to his mind, superior Anglo-Saxon culture" (Talbot 198).
2. In Norman Shapiro's translation, *seigneur* becomes squire.
3. See Boudreau, p. 309-11.
4. In his chapter on Quebec in the book *Genèse des nations et cultures du Nouveau Monde: Essie d'histoire comparée*, Gérard Bouchard outlines the two major lines of Quebec history and culture: the elite and the popular. Popular culture was full of myths and traditions, such as

"contes," which told secular, magical tales of the days of the "courreurs de bois."

5. See Bouchard, 2001.

6. See Fortier, p. 68 for an explanation of how some of the symbolic of this nickname is lost in the translation.

BIBLIOGRAPHY

Bouchard, Gérard. *Genèse des nations et cultures du Nouveau Monde: Essai d'histoire comparée.* Montreal: Boréal, 2001.

Boudreau, Douglas L. "Anglophone Presence in the Early Novels of Anne Hébert." *The French Review.* 74.2 (2000): 308-318.

Cohen, Henry. "The Role of Myth in Anne Hébert's *Kamouraska.*" Chitra Reddin, trans. *Essays on Canadian Writing.* 10 (1978): 134-143.

Côté, Paul Raymond. "*Kamouraska* ou l'influence d'une tradition." *The French Review.* 63.1 (1989): 99-111.

Fortier, Shirley. "(Non)inscription du féminin dans la traduction anglaise de *Kamouraska.*" *Cahiers Anne Hébert.* 3 (2001): 63-76.

Green, Mary Jean. "Dismantling the Colonizing Text: Anne Hébert's *Kamouraska* and Assia Djebar's *L'Amour, la fantasie.*" *The French Review.* 66.6 (1993): 959-66.

Hébert, Anne. *Kamouraska.* Paris: Seuil, 1970

——. *Kamouraska.* Norman Shapiro, trans. Toronto: General, 1982.

——. *Oeuvre poétique: 1950-1990.* Montreal: Boréal, 1993.

Lemieux, Pierre-Hervé. "La Mort des rois: Commentaire du poème-titre "Le Tombeau des rois" d'Anne Hébert." *Revue de l'Université d'Ottawa* 45.2 (1975) 133-161.

——. *Entre songe et parle: Structure du "Tombeau des rois" d'Anne Hébert.* Ottawa: Éditions de l'Université d'Ottawa, 1978.

——. "Le Tombeau des rois." *Dictionnaire des oeuvres Lit-*

téraires du Québec. Tome III. Montreal: Fides, 1978. 1940-1959.

Les Patriotes de 1837-1838. http://www.cvm.qc.ca/patriotes/index2.shtml

Pascal-Ssmith, Gabrielle. "La Condition féminine dans *Kamouraska* d'Anne Hébert." *The French Review*. 54.1 (1980): 85-92.

Pelletier, Sylvain. "Soi tout autre. Le docteur Nelson dans *Kamouraska* d'Anne Hébert." *Cahiers Anne Hébert*. 1 (1999): 29-45.

Rose, Marilyn Gaddis. "When an Author Chooses French: Hébert and Chedid." *Québec Studies*. 3 (1985): 148-59.

Smart, Patricia. *Writing in the Father's House: The Emergence of the Feminine in the Quebec Literary Tradition*. Toronto: UTP, 1991.

——. "La poèsie d'Anne Hébert: une perspective féministe." L'autre lecture: La critique au féminin et les textes québécois." Tome 1. Ed. Lori Saint-Martin. Montreal: XYZ éditeur, 1992.

Talbot, Émile J. "The Signifying Absence: Reading *Kamouraska* Politically." *Canadian Literature*. 130 (1991): 194-200.

Z-shek, Ben. "Diaglossia and Ideology: Socio-Cultural Aspects of "Translation" in Quebec." *TTR: Traduction, Terminologie, Rédaction*. 1.1 (1988): 85-91.

Zecher, Carla. "Elisabeth-*Sainte* and Aurélie-*Sorcière*: The Mistress of Kamouraska and Her Double." *Quebec Studies*. 20 (1995): 11-18.

Anne Hébert: Interview

Michel Gosselin

The following interview was the final one before her death in 2000. It was originally published in French, in *Cahiers Anne Hébert*, Number 2 (2000), and was conducted by Michel Gosselin. The interview has been translated by the editor of this volume and is reprinted with Michel Gosselin's permission.

M.G. Over the past few years, your books have appeared with increasing frequency. Whereas before it would take three or four years for a new work to appear, now it's closer to being a yearly occurrence. How do you explain this shift?

A.H. I think that, when you're younger, life takes up more of your time. I have a lot more free time for writing now as opposed to when I was younger. As time goes by, and I get older, I have to let go of those things that no longer fit. Gone are those long trips, literary tours, small dinner parties that I would prepare for some friends, going to market or shopping. What has happened to those friends whom I used to hold so closely?

M.G. Has writing for you gotten easier – a certain confidence that comes with practice – or is it still as much work as when you described it in "Écrire un poème" [*Poèmes* 1960]?

A.H. I believe that I have the same difficulties I have always had, as I have always tried to avoid redoing the same type of piece, tried not to wade into the same pool, and so each time it's starting from scratch. For me, it cannot become routine. And if that were to unfortunately happen, something like habitual writing, it would represent, to me, a negation of the creative process itself. Writing a book is a new adventure in uncharted territory each time. Understand that we are never able to separate from ourselves. There is always something new to discover deeper within ourselves, something that has not been said and needs to be expressed in words. It's at once joyous and terrifying.

M.G. But a habit of writing must help somewhat?

A.H. No, nothing is gained in advance, as I said. Each time, you start fresh.

M.G. Is the energy of where you work important? Does it influence, in that moment, what you are writing?

A.H. I am just as comfortable writing in Paris as I am in Montreal. External places do not exist for me when I write . . .nor the weather outside. For me, writing is a closed circuit between myself and the pages in front of me. What are created are places and landscapes that I already know and possess. I call on the angels and demons already living inside of me, who are created, little by little, over many days and nights, in the depths of my flesh and blood.

M.G. Places that you have already possessed?

A.H. Exactly. I have to be a part of the places. The places must fit with the characters. It would never occur to me to take a character that I knew elsewhere and put them in a place that I do not know.

M.G. Since you have returned to Quebec, a place that you never completely left given the importance in the setting of your works, have you felt your imagination drifting towards different landscapes than the ones you have invited readers to inhabit?

A.H. People forget that *Les Chambres de bois* takes place in France, not in Canada, as many have thought. *Héloïse* also takes place in France, specifically in Paris.

M.G. After reading the body of your writings, it would seem to me that with *Aurélien, Clara, Mademoiselle et le lieutenant anglais* you finished a long cycle that dealt with disconnected childhood. Having Clara go to the English lieutenant would seem to indicate, for the first time in your stories, that the young character has decided for herself to leave the comfortable world of childhood where nothing happens and jump feet-first into the adult world?

A.H. I think that the story of Clara and the English lieutenant, for me, does finish a preoccupation of a certain terrain I've been exploring since *Le Torrent*. I believe I've said all there is to say about that terrain, I lived it, I loved it with all of my being, but without a doubt I am leaving a place that has given to me all of its secrets about life and death.

M.G. Is there sometimes a danger that to the detriment of the text the narrator may get carried away with gratuitous images?

A.H. You always have to be vigilant, not to let yourself get caught up in the sweetness. A beautiful sentence for the sake of a beautiful sentence. At first glance, because there are two, when you look at the work, you're wrapped up in it. But the second time, which is more critical, and you see these gratuitous beautiful sentences, you must remove them.

M.G. How do you think these temptations come about? Through an easily written ending? Through a character's or story's clumsy logic?

A.H. Understand that there are always surprises. Certain parts of a story can escape you. It's only after rereading, after having written the whole text, that you can see certain errors, certain things that haven't been tied up properly or are badly presented. They don't happen naturally. So they have to be removed, changed.

M.G. Do you find it difficult to remove a sentence that you think is beautiful, but it doesn't fit in the story?

A.H. Yes, but I really believe in the whole. It weighs on me in the moment, but I know that I have to take it out of the story.

M.G. Does the subject of the story come to you first or is it the need to write that drives you over and above the subject matter?

A.H. I think I have two views on this subject: either you need to write, or you don't need to write. When you need to write, the subject becomes available to you to a certain point. The subject of a story is like a stranger who knocks on your door and whispers to you. The characters rush in with the subject, with the door barely opened, all pushing and demanding to be heard. Sometimes it's the beginning of a long tale of tumult and jubilation between the subject and the characters, leading into an intimate and deep union that becomes a book. And sometimes the story and the characters rebel along the way, go silent, distort their face. Stillborn, they return to the land of the dead, where they should never have left.

M.G. So you believe that openness, a state of grace would perhaps be the conditions so that the subject may come forward?

A.H. You have to be open to love, a love that fades. There are moments when you meet someone and they have all the possible qualities — they should make you happy, but you aren't attracted to them at all because you don't possess that openness within yourself.

M.G. Has it happened that you think you have found a good subject, but after a few pages of writing, you become aware that it's not working?

A.H. I've often had false starts, but I've often started over again. For example, I had started a first draft of *Les Fous de Bassan*; at about 50 pages in it wasn't working. I came back to *Les Fous de Bassan* after I had realized that I had distanced myself too much from my characters by trying to tell the story in the third person, a bit like a journalist writing about some current event.

M.G. But in general, when you start writing a text, you have a good handle on your subject, and the fervor helps . . .

A.H. You forget that there is a lot of work involved. Fervor isn't enough. For *Un habit de lumière*, I did three versions.

M.G. Is it important that you are satisfied with your work, that it be almost perfect?

A.H. Yes, it's like an attempt at an absolute that will never be realized. You have to place the bar as high as possible even if it will never be reached.

M.G. Up until now, you've received a number of literary prizes and distinctions. Are these rewards important to a writer?

A.H. The literary prizes and distinctions that I have received throughout my career were of great help to me, both morally and materially. What a great comfort to think that the message in a bottle thrown out to sea with such apprehension and anxiety was well received! Moreover, living by the pen and making writing your job isn't always easy. Often, small tokens don't suffice. The Molson prize, for example, allowed me to finish *Kamouraska* in relative security. I would say that, for me, the rewards and prizes were absolutely vital.

M.G. In your last novel, *Un habit de lumière*, you address a new issue that we don't find in your previous works, the question of sexual identity. While Rose-Alba dreams of her son Miguel wearing the suit of light of a toreador, this seven-year-old boy dreams of a luxurious house and announces to his mother: "I am waiting for my husband!"

A.H. Miguel is a homosexual, but especially a transsexual. These are subjects that we are talking a lot about lately. Discussing the operation and all that on the radio, on television. This female athlete became a man, this actor or actress.

M.G. In *Un habit de lumière*, there are no Canadian characters at all. Why? Do you not feel the need to create Canadian or Québécois characters?

A.H. I am drawn to and passionate about living beings, be they Quebecois, French, or Spanish. My task is to find in each of them what makes them human and unique. I'm looking for their solitary soul, hidden under the external appearances of a caste or nationality. For little Miguel, like all of my other characters, I try to make him live with all of his contradictions and his frantic desire to be recognized, out in the open, for who he really is in all of his difference and his wounded heart. As for your second question, the story would have to have taken place in Quebec. But seeing as I lived for so long in France, and I knew concierges since the 1950s, many of who are immigrant workers . . .

M.G. . . .you felt the need to write on that subject.

A.H. I felt close to them.

M.G. Their thirst to escape from misery?

A.H. Yes, from their misery. Rose-Alba thinks only of money, of looking like stars such as Lady Diana or Claudia Schiffer. It's a phenomenon of modern life, that people dream only of a world of artifice.

M.G. A world of artifice that Rose-Alba finds at the *Paradis Perdu*?

A.H. At the *Paradis Perdu* in all its flashiness.

M.G. In your novel, young Miguel and his mother both desire the same person, Jean-Éphrem de la Tour, or the Angel of Darkness as put by the son. I found it audacious that you would have the son and the mother share the same desire. What do you think?

A.H. From the beginning, the mother desires Jean-Éphrem. When she sees him backstage, in a large towel, in a sheet, she finds him attractive. And then her son keeps talking about the infamous loft where there are chairs of gold and walls of velvet. To her, it becomes more beautiful than the *Paradis Perdu*. Really, she's a seductress. She wants to sleep with him.

M.G. She's a seductress, even though she knows her son desires the same man as she does?

A.H. Life is always more audacious than literature. Why wouldn't a boy and his mother fall in love with the same man in real life? And isn't the source of the novel life at its most raw and naked? There are no taboo subjects, and life belongs to everyone, even the writers.

M.G. You are an author who has influenced, is influencing and will influence still more generations of writers of poetry and prose. How do you feel about being one of Quebec literature's leading writers? Is it a responsibility that you find difficult, or is it one that you readily embrace?

A.H. I think that the first responsibility of the writer is to write. And if you're honest with yourself, you accept it readily. No matter that you've influenced someone, it's if you've done it as honestly as possible. The first responsibility that I fully embrace is to write without compromise, which I've done my whole life.

M.G. Do you find that the literature being written in Quebec at the moment has changed a lot since you started writing? I'm thinking in particular of the theme of religion that appears in the majority of novels from a certain period.

A.H. I think that Quebec has changed, and it's normal that her literature has changed too.

M.G. It's a literature that is following the times?

A.H. Yes, it's following the times more and more closely. Before, there was really a large gap between the literature from France and the literature from Quebec, which has finally become a modern literature. Before Gabrielle Roy and Roger Lemelin, it was always going back to the land. Those are the two novelists who started to write urban novels. Poetry, on the other hand, preceded the novel into modernity with Saint-Denys Garneay, Alain Grandbois and Rina Lasnier.

M.G. One final question Madame Hébert. The Université de Sherbrooke has established the Centre Anne-Hébert and assures, among other things, continuity to your work through organizing conferences, seminars, symposiums, etc . . . Could you explain to me how you see the importance of this to the students who will be studying your works?

A.H. The research and study Centre that carries my name at the Université de Sherbrooke is particularly touching to me, and allows me to dream of a second life for my works, over time, as time will eventually run out on me. As for what I hope students find interesting, the desire for exactness that all work that is well done demands.

M.G. Like what Boileau wrote in his *Art poétique*?

A.H. I agree with exactness, but not with monsieur Boileau.

M.G. Madame Hébert, I thank you.

Biography of Anne Hébert

Born in 1916 near Quebec City, Hébert benefited from a world where she was encouraged to read and imagine.[1] Her father was a respected poet and a high-ranking bureaucrat, insulating the family against the censorship imposed by the Catholic Church during much of the early twentieth century. She was of noble blood on her mother's side: a direct descendent of Eugène-Étienne Taché, architect for the Quebec parliament building, and Achille Taché, Seigneur (Lord) of Kamouraska. Her cousin, poet Hector de Saint-Denys Garneau, also influenced young Hébert, introducing her to modern French poets and poetry. Although she wrote throughout her adolescence, particularly plays that would be performed for friends and family, her first collection of poems, *Les Songes en équilibre*, only appeared in 1942. The collection was well received and came third for the Prix Athanase-David. Over the next ten years, Hébert would publish a number of plays and short stories, including *Le Torrent* in 1950. She also worked at Radio-Canada and the National Film Board, writing and producing scripts and radio plays.

While *Le Torrent* and her second collection of poems (*Le Tombeau des rois*) were critically successful, Hébert had a great deal of difficulty finding publishers for her work. Intense censorship and repression led the author to France, where, in 1958, she finished writing, and immediately found a publisher for, her first novel (*Les chambres de bois*). The manuscript won the Prix de l'Association France-Canada and the Prix Athanase-David. Two years later, *Poèmes* was published, earning Hébert her first Governor-General's Award. Over the next ten years, Hébert split her time between Quebec and France, finally settling in Paris upon the death of her mother in 1965. Hébert would publish another play, *Le temps sauvage* (1967), as well as another edition of *Le Torrent* (1963), which included two new short stories. In 1967, Hébert received the Prix Molson from the Canada Council for the Arts for the body of her work.

The year 1970 saw the publication of her most celebrated novel, *Kamouraska*. The novel is partially based on a murder involving members of her family. Winning both the Prix des Libraires de France and the Prix de littérature hors de France de l'Académie royale de Belgique, Hébert firmly established herself as an important and influential author on both sides of the Atlantic, as well as ensuring her financial security. Prior to the novel becoming a bestseller, Hébert was dependant on small grants from both the Federal and Provincial governments in Canada, and selling stories to magazines. Claude Jutra bought the film rights and directed the movie version of the novel, which was a modest box office success. In 1975, Hébert published her third novel, *Les Enfants du sabbat*, earning the author another Governor-General Award and the Prix de l'Académie française. She continued writing radio plays, with *L'Île de la Demoiselle* being performed in 1978.

In 1980, Hébert published *Héloise*, and *Les Fous de Bassan* in 1982 – the latter novel earned her the Prix

Fémina, one of France's highest literary honors. One year later, she would be awarded an honorary doctorate from Université Laval, the fifth she would receive over her career. *Le premier jardin* would appear in 1988. In 1990, Hébert would publish another play, *La cage* and in 1992, her first collection of poetry in more than thirty years, *Le jour n'a d'égal que la nuit*, appeared, along with the novel *L'enfant chargé de songes*, which would win yet another Governor-General Award. Between 1990 and her death on January 22, 2000, she would publish one play, two collections of poetry, and four novels, including *Aurélien, Clara, Mademoiselle et le Lieutenant anglais* (1995), *Poèmes pour la main gauche* (1997), *Est-ce que je te dérange?* (1998) and *Un habit de lumière* (1999). In 1998, Hébert also decided to move back to Quebec, after living for over thirty years in Paris.

An intensely private person, Hébert never married, nor had any children. She devoted her life to her writing, and the result is one of the most important literary careers in Canada. Her works are all staggering in their poetic quality, as well as their fearlessness. Hébert was never afraid to treat difficult or challenging subjects in her writing, and as often dove into the depths of human suffering and depravity as she did lift us to see the beauty and light of our existence. In May 2000, the Prix Anne-Hébert was created, and is awarded annually to the best first novel written in French from Canada.

1. Much of biographical information has been taken from the following sources: Robert Harvey's website (http://www.anne-hebert.com/index.html), the site for the Center Anne-Hébert, Université de Sherbrooke (http://www.usherbrooke.ca/centreanne-hebert/) and Janet M. Paterson's entry for Hébert in the *Encyclopedia of Literature in Canada*, edited by W.H. New, 2002.

Bibliography

Works by Anne Hébert:

Les Songes en équilibre: Montréal, Les Editions de L'Arbre, 1942.

Le Torrent. Montréal: Beauchemin, 1950. Montréal: HMH, coll. L'Arbre, 1963. Montreal: Bibliothèque Québécoise(BQ), 1989. Introduction by Robert Harvey.

Le Tombeau des rois. Québec: Institut littéraire du Québec, 1953. Preface by Pierre Emmanuel.

Les Chambres de bois. Paris: Ed. du Seuil, 1958. Preface by Samuel de Sacy.

Poèmes. Paris: Ed. du Seuil, 1960. Preface by Pierre Emmanuel.

Le Temps sauvage. Montréal: HMH, coll. L'Arbre, 1967. Montréal: BQ, 1992. Introduction by Robert Harvey.

Dialogue sur la traduction à propos du Tombeau des rois. Montréal: HMH, 1970. Montréal: BQ, 2000. With Frank Scott. Presentation by Jeanne Lapointe. Preface by Northrop Frye.

Kamouraska. Paris: Ed. du Seuil, 1970.

Les Enfants du sabbat. Paris: Ed. du Seuil, 1975.

Héloïse. Paris: Ed. du Seuil, 1980.

Les Fous de Bassan. Paris: Ed. du Seuil, 1982.

Le Premier jardin. Paris: Ed. du Seuil, 1988.

La Cage, suivi de *L'Île de la Demoiselle.* Montréal/Paris: Boréal/Seuil, 1990.

L'Enfant chargé de songes. Paris: Ed. du Seuil, 1992.

Le Jour n'a d'égal que la nuit. Montréal/Paris: Boréal/Seuil, 1992.

Œuvre poétique (1950-1990). Montréal/Paris: Boréal/Seuil, Boréal compact no 40, 1993.

Aurélien, Clara, Mademoiselle et le Lieutenant anglais. Paris: Ed. du Seuil, 1995.

Poèmes pour la main gauche. Montréal: Boréal, 1997.

Est-ce que je te dérange? Paris: Ed. du Seuil, 1998.

Un habit de lumière. Paris: Ed. du Seuil, 1999.

English Translations

The Tomb of Kings. Trans. Peter Miller. Toronto: Contact Press, 1967.

The Torrent. Trans. Gwendolyn Moore. Montreal: Harvest House, 1973.

The Silent Rooms. Trans. Kathy Mezei. Don Mills, Ont: Musson, 1974.

Kamouraska. Trans. Norman Shapiro. Don Mills, Ont: PaperJacks, 1974. Toronto: General, 1982. Toronto: Anansi, 2000.

Poems. Trans. Alan Brown. Don Mills, Ont: Musson, 1975.

Children of the Black Sabbath. Trans. Carol Dunlop-Hébert. Don Mills, Ont: Musson, 1977.

Héloïse. Trans. Sheila Fischman. Toronto: Stoddart, 1982. Toronto: General, 1983.

In the Shadow of the Wind. Trans. Sheila Fischman. Toronto: General, 1984. Toronto: Anansi, 1994.

Anne Hébert: Selected Poems. Trans. Alfred Poulin Jr. Brockport, NY: BOA, 1987.

The First Garden. Trans. Sheila Fischman. Toronto: Anansi, 1990.

The Burden of Dreams. Trans. Sheila Fischman. Toronto: Anansi, 1994.

Day Has No Equal but Night. Trans. Alfred Poulin Jr. Brockport, NY: 1994.

Aurélien, Clara, Mademoiselle, and the English Lieutenant. Trans. Sheila Fischman. Toronto: Anansi, 1996.

Day Has No Equal but the Night. Trans. Lola Lemire
   Tostevin. Toronto: Anansi, 1997.
Am I disturbing you? Trans. Sheila Fischman. Toronto:
   Anansi, 1999.
A Suit of Light. Trans. Sheila Fischman. Toronto: Anansi,
   2000.
Collected Later Novels. Trans. Sheila Fischman. Toronto:
   Anansi, 2003. Introduction by Mavis Gallant.

Publications about Anne Hébert

In 2001, Janis L. Pallister edited a book of essays on Anne
Hébert, *Night and the Day are One: The Art and Genius of
Anne Hébert: Essays on Her Works*. The book contains an
extensive bibliography, one of the most complete put together. The following bibliography is meant to complimentary,
including all works published after the release date of Pallister's book.

Boisclair, Isabelle. "Aliénation identitaires, alienation
   économiques dans *Un Habit de lumière*," *Voix et Images*
   29.1 (2003): 115-27.
Briand, Sylvie. "*Les Fous de Bassan* d'Anne Hébert ou
   l'apocalypse du griffon," *Études Françaisesi* 36.2 (2000):
   149-62.
Colvile, Georgiana. "Anti-fleuves, corps morcelés, identités
   fracassées: *Le Torrent* d'Anne Hébert (1950) et *The
   Whirlpool* de Jane Urquhart (1986)," *Canadian Studies*
   50 (2001): 157-65.
Gasse, Julie. "Pour une poétique de secret dans l'oeuvre
   d'Anne Hébert," *Tangence* 62 (2000): 139-44.
Green, Mary Jean. "The Witch and the Princess: The Feminine Fantastic in the Fiction of Anne Hébert," *Women
   Writing in Quebec*. Ed. Paula Ruth Gilbert et al. Plattsburgh, NY: Center for the Study of Canada: 2000. 62-73.

Kellett-Betsos, Kathleen. "La Fugue, la fuite et l'espace franchi dans *Le premier jardin* d'Anne Hébert," *Studies in Canadian Literature* 29.1 (2004): 50-62.

Lord, Michel. "Entre le sec et l'humide: Les Signes de l'ambivalence dans *Les Fous de Bassan* d'Anne Hébert," *Frontières flottantes: Lieu et espace dans les cultures francophones du Canada*. Ed. Jaap Lintvelt et al. Amsterdam: Rodopi, 2001. 191-203.

Lyngaas, Scott. "Eve in the New World: The Search for the Origins in Anne Hébert's *Le premier jardin*," *Cincinnati Romance Review* 21 (2002): 50-60.

Marcheix, Daniel. "Pratique des signes et fascination de l'informe dans les romans d'Anne Hébert," *Voix et Images* 27.2 (2002): 317-36.

Marchese, Elena. "*Le premier jardin* d'Anne Hébert et *La maison Trestler* de Madeleine Ouellette-Michalska: Deux examples de réécriture historique qui renouvellent le concept d'Histoire," *Studies in Canadian Literature* 27.1 (2002): 105-19.

Mitchell, Constantina. "La symbolique de la surdité dans *Le Torrent* d'Anne Hébert," *Women Writing in Quebec*. Ed. Paula Ruth Gilbert et al. Plattsburgh, NY: Center for the Study of Canada: 2000. 53-61.

Mondenesi, Marco. "Anne Hébert et l'espace parisien," *L'Europe de la culture québécoise*. Ed. Jean-Paul Dufiet et al. Udine. Italy: Forum, 2002. 49-58.

Mongeon, Sylvie. "Le Frôlement de l'impossible dans l'oeuvre d'Anne Hébert," *Métamorphoses: Réflexions critiques sur la literature, la langue et le cinema*. Ed. Kirsty Bell et al. Toronto: Paratexte, 2002. 7-14.

Noble, Peter. "Anne Hébert: *Kamouraska* and *Les Fous de Bassan*," *Where are the Voices Coming From? Canadian Culture and the Legacies of History*. Ed. Coral Ann Howells. Amsterdam: Rodopi, 2004. 39-54.

Ouellet, Julie. "La Rhétorique de l'idiot," *Études littéraires* 33.2 (2001): 169-85.

Pallister, Janis L. ed. *Night and Day are One: The Art and Genius of Anne Hébert: Essays on her Works.* Madison: Fairleigh Dickinson UP; London: Associated UP, 2001.

Pouzet, Virginie. "*Le Tombeau des rois* d'Anne Hébert: Des dualité aux symboles," *South Carolina Modern Languages Review* 2.1 (2003): n.p.

Purdy, Anthony. "Unearthing the Past: The Archeology of the Bog Bodies in Glob, Atwood, Hébert and Drabble," *Textual Practices* 16.3 (2002): 443-458.

Rea, Annabelle M. "Marie-Josephte Becomes Ludivine: The Family Reformed in Anne Hébert's *La Cage*," *Doing Gender: Franco-Canadian Women Writers of the 1990s*. Ed. Roseanna L. Dufault. Madison, NJ: Fairleigh Dickinson UP, 2001. 23-35.

Rimstead, Roxanne. "Working-Class Intruders: Female Domestics in *Kamouraska* and *Alias Grace*," *Canadian Literature* 175 (2002): 44-65.

Saint-Martin, Lori. "Inventer la mémoire," *Voix et Images* 28.2 (2003): 191-97.

Tulloch, Elspeth. "Yves Simoneau's Rewriting of the Troubled Manhood Script in Anne Hébert's *Les Fous de Bassan*," *Essays on Canadian Writing* 76 (2002): 83-116.

Vandervoort, Edith. "When They Were Young: Adolescent Representations in *Les Fous de Bassan*," *Québec Studies* 36 (2004): 69-81.

Books on Anne Hébert

Arcrenat, Anne-Marie. *De mémoire de femmes: "la mémoire archaïque" dans l'ouevre romanesque d'Anne Hébert.* Québec: Nota bene, 2002.

Bishop, Neil. *Anne Hébert, son oeuvre, leurs exils.* Boudeaux: Presses universitaires de Bordeaux, 1993.

Bouchard, Denis. *Une lecture d'Anne Hébert: La recherché d'une mythologie.* Montreal: Hurtubise HMH, 1977.

Brochu, André. *Anne Hébert, Le secret de vie et de mort*. Ottawa: Ottawa UP, 2000.

Cassista, Claude. *Claude Cassista et Jean Simard présentent* Le Torrent *d'Anne Hébert*. Montréal: Leméac, 2001.

Demers, Sylvie. Le Torrent *d'Anne Hébert*. Montréal: Hurtubise HMH, 1998.

Ducrocq-Poirier, Madelaine et al. *Anne Hébert, parcours d'une oeuvre. Colloque de Paris III et Paris IV-Sorbonne, mai 1996*. Montréal: Hexagone, 1997.

Emond, Maurice. *Le récit comme fil d'Ariane*. Québec: Nota bene, 2000.

———. *La femme à la fenêtre*. Québec: PUL, 1984.

Harvey, Robert. *Poétique d'Anne Hébert: jeunesse et genèse, suivi de Lecture du Tombeau des rois*. Québec: L'instant meme, 2000.

———. *Kamouraska d'Anne Hébert: une écriture de la passion, suivi de Pour un nouveau* Torrent. Montréal: Hurtubise HMH, 1982.

Lacôte, René. *Anne Hébert*. Paris: Seghers, 1969.

Lemieux, Pierre-Hervé. *Entre songe et parole. Structure du* Tombeau des rois *d'Anne Hébert*. Ottawa: Ottawa UP, 1978.

Marcheix, Daniel. *Le mal d'origine: temps et identité dans l'oeuvre romanesque d'Anne Hébert*. Québec: L'Instant meme, 2005.

Major, Jean-Louis. *Anne Hébert et le Miracle de la parole*. Montréal: PUM, 1976.

Mitchell, Constantina. *Textual Interplay in the fiction of Maraux, Hébert, and Modiano*. Providence: Berghahn Books, 1996.

Nazir Garant, France. *Eve et le cheval de grève: contribution à l'étude de l'imaginaire d'Anne Hébert*. Québec: PUL, 1988.

Page, Pierre. *Anne Hébert*. Montréal: Fides, 1965.

Paterson, Janet M. *Anne Hébert. Architexture romanesque*. Ottawa: Ottawa UP, 1985.

Robert, Guy. *La poétique du songe: introduction à l'oeuvre d'Anne Hébert*. Montreal: Association générale des étudiants de l'Université de Montréal, 1962.

Roy, Lucille. *Entre la lumière et l'ombre: l'univers poétique d'Anne Hébert*. Sherbrooke: Naaman, 1984.

Russel, Delbert W. *Anne Hébert*. Boston: Twane, 1983.

Thériault, Serge A. *La quête d'équilibre dan l'oeuvre romanesque d'Anne Hébert*. Hull: Éditions Asticou, 1980.

Wyczynski, Paul. *Poésie et symbole: perspectives du symbolisme; Emile Nelligan; Saint-Denys Garneau; Anne Hébert; Le langage des arbres*. Montréal: Librarie Déom, 1965.

Websites and Other References

http://www.anne-hebert.com/
The complete site for Hébert in French.
http://www.usherbrooke.ca/biblio/catalo/
http://www.usherbrooke.ca/centreanne-hebert/
The site for the Centre Anne-Hébert and the Université de Sherbrooke library where you can search through the entire archives and documents found at the Centre Anne-Hébert
http://www.usherbrooke.ca/centreanne-hebert/cahier/*Les Cahiers Anne-Hébert*

Contributors

Deborah Hamilton has a B.A. in French from the University of California, Berkeley; and an M.A. in French from Middlebury College, where she wrote her master's thesis on "Aspects of Light and Dark in Anne Hébert's *Aurélien, Clara, Mademoiselle, and the English Lieutenant* and Marguerite Duras' *Emily L.*" She has lived in Paris and is interested in contemporary women's literature.

Michel Gosselin is a writer and teacher living in Sherbrooke, Quebec. He has written for numerous mediums, including radio and television. He is one of the founders of the Grand Prix littéraires de la Ville de Sherbrooke, as well as the Centre Anne-Hébert.

Bénédicte N. Mauguière, Professor (Doctorat, Université Paris IV-Sorbonne), BORSF Endowed Professor of Francophone Studies (2002-2005) teaches Francophone Studies at the University of Louisiana at Lafayette with a focus on Canadian Studies and the French East Indies. She is the Director of the Conseil International d'Etudes Francophones (CIEF), the largest academic association in Francophone Studies worldwide. She has an extensive record of research and publications with two books: *Cultural Identities in Canadian Literature* (NY: Peter Lang, 1998); *Traversée des idéologies et exploration des identités dans les écritures de femmes au Québec,1970-1980* (NY: Peter Lang, 1997) and numerous peer-reviewed publications in University presses and academic journals (*Quebec Studies, The French Review, Présence Francophone, Cahiers Anne Hébert, Etudes Francophones, Cahiers internationaux de symbolisme*).

Annabelle M. Rea, Professor of French Emerita at Occidental College in Los Angeles, began working on Anne Hébert in 1983, thanks to a grant from the Quebec government. She has published numerous articles on

Hébert, as well as on George Sand. As Chair of Women in French from 1990 to 1995, she dedicated herself to the promotion of women writers in general. Currently, she serves as President of the George Sand Association and as a member of the Editorial Board of *George Sand Studies*.

Dr Elodie Rousselot works at the University of Kent, United Kingdom. She was the recipient of the Prix du Québec in 2002 and of the International Council for Canadian Studies Graduate Student Thesis Scholarship in 2001. Her publications include a number of works on Anne Hébert, as well as Quebec literature in general. Her current research project focuses on contemporary Anglophone and francophone Canadian female novelists and the writing of historical fiction.

Lee Skallerup has a Ph.D in Comparative Literature from the University of Alberta. She was introduced to the poetry of Anne Hébert as an undergraduate student at the Université de Sherbrooke, and the author has fascinated her ever since. Ms. Skallerup has also published on authors Dany Laferrière, Mordecai Richler and Nalo Hopkinson. She is an assistant professor at Florida A&M University.

Robert David Stacey teaches Canadian literature in the Department of English at York University. Most of his recent work explores the ideological implications of literary form. He has presented and published on a number of Canadian authors including P.K. Page, Leonard Cohen, John Steffler, Jacques Poulin, and William Kirby.

Printed in July 2010
at Gauvin Press,
Gatineau, Québec